THE VISCOTT METHOD

A REVOLUTIONARY PROGRAM FOR SELF-ANALYSIS AND SELF-UNDERSTANDING

DAVID VISCOTT M.D.

POCKET BOOKS

New York   London   Toronto   Sydney   Tokyo

To that better world
Where all people are free to give their best,
Where peace replaces chaos,
And love triumphs over greed.

POCKET BOOKS, a division of Simon & Schuster, Inc.
1230 Avenue of the Americas, New York, N.Y. 10020

Copyright © 1984 by David Viscott

Published by arrangement with Houghton Mifflin Company
Library of Congress Catalog Card Number: 83-12778

ISBN: 0-671-67088-3

First Pocket Books printing April 1985

10 9 8 7 6 5 4

POCKET and colophon are trademarks of
Simon & Schuster, Inc.

Cover art based on a design © American Greetings Corporation

Cover design by Amy King

Printed in the U.S.A.

"Your life should always be getting better.

You should prosper and feel good about it. You should know joy and love. . . .

In this book I will show you how to resolve your life's pain so that you can experience its joy and pleasure fully. . . . The growth techniques revealed here define a natural therapy through living honestly. They will teach you how to create your best life. . . ."

—*Dr. David Viscott*

DAVID VISCOTT, M.D., bestselling author of *The Making of a Psychiatrist, How to Live with Another Person,* and *Risking,* is a graduate of Tufts University Medical School. He has taught at Boston University Medical School and served as Senior Psychiatrist and consultant for the State of Massachusetts. Dr. Viscott currently hosts his own weekly radio show in Los Angeles, "David Viscott's Saturday Night," during which he answers questions from listeners about psychiatry and self-fulfillment. He is the father of three children and lives in Los Angeles with his wife, Katherine Random.

I know of no more
encouraging fact than the
unquestionable ability of man
to elevate his life by a
conscious endeavor.

—Henry David Thoreau, *Walden*

Contents

To Those Seeking Happiness

All my life I've been looking for answers. All my life I've been making mistakes. Sometimes I'd look for love where no love was to be found, and for years I tried to substitute duty and obligation for my own personal fulfillment. I struggled to find myself in a career that only partly satisfied my creative needs. I wanted to be a musician or a writer, but my father, a pharmacist who wanted to be a doctor, had other ideas. I was not strong or sure enough to believe I could survive myself. It was easy to blame my father, but the truth was that even without the pressure to go to medical school, I lacked the drive to pursue what I loved because I feared testing my ability.

I married my childhood sweetheart, partly out of love and partly out of a youthful sense of responsibility that was brought to a head when her parents were killed in an automobile accident after dropping her off to visit me at Dartmouth. Although my wife and I were good friends and shared many interests, we still felt unfulfilled. In an effort to find ourselves, my wife re-newed her passion for figure skating and I started writing and studying music again. Not surprisingly, as we grew, we also grew apart.

I found success and fulfillment in my writing, met a woman one afternoon in a ski line in Vermont, fell in love, got divorced and moved from Boston to California, remarried, and started the life I had always wanted to lead.

So you want to talk about freeing yourself from guilt, dealing with people who act out their frustrations and conflicts, coping with the death of parents, the anger of family, the envy of friends, and the manipulations and abuses of lovers? I've seen it all and lived through it by facing my problems as directly and honestly as I could.

I haven't just survived. I've lived the happiest, most productive years of my life, and most of the time I've been optimistic and creative. There is no secret to surviving happily. The best way to cope is to live through pain and experience it. If you hide from your feelings, the problems that caused them remain unresolved. Held in and allowed to fester, pain becomes suffering and hurt builds into seething anger. It's far better to experience your pain completely, to let go of it when you're done, to give up what is lost and move on. Otherwise, your life becomes directed from forces in your past that still seek expression and you are not free to live, to enjoy, or to be yourself.

To be open is best.

I believe this with all my heart. I teach this to my patients. I try to live this way because it makes me feel best.

Life is not supposed to be any special way in particular. Life is only what you make of it. Whether or not you realize it or take responsibility for it, you are constantly creating your own life. In the end, you get pretty much what you give. So nothing much changes unless you want it to or until you do something about it.

You can go through life seeking negative evidence that undermines you, hiding in fear that the worst will probably happen. And sure enough, it does. Or you can seek the support that gives you the courage to risk in the hope that the best will happen to you. And if you work at it, it usually does.

The way you are is the way your world is.

Solving the mystery of your own life is a task that is yours alone. Of course, you can avoid the question entirely. You can pass through life as if in a dream, but then your life will lack depth and quickly become boring. Or you can seek to understand how you create the world you live in, take charge, and start building a life that fulfills you. If you don't, it probably won't happen. You can feel cheated if you want, but you'll have no one to blame but yourself.

Your life should always be getting better. You should prosper and feel good about it. You should know joy and love. You should suffer all your sorrows their portion in their proper time to be free to contribute your part and be happy.

A full life processes all its experiences honestly. Events do not occur suddenly without warning, nor are they forgotten without a trace. Every emotion must run its course. Each loss must bear its hurt. Every anger must find its peace. The story of your life is told in the voice of the emotions you felt as you were living it. A rich life has its full share of positive and negative emotions. The difference between a happy life and an unhappy one is in the way each person comes to terms with pain. The pain of life must be processed: the fear trembled, the sadness felt, the anger quickened, and guilt mourned.

In this book I will show you how to resolve your life's pain so that you can experience its joy and pleasure fully. When sad events are not resolved, they live on to contaminate what is good and lessen your optimism. The growth techniques revealed here define a natural therapy through living honestly. It will teach you how to create your best life.

Its object is to make you free.

David Viscott, M.D.
Los Angeles, California

1 | The Method

This is an adventure into the world within you to help you to comprehend the forces that drive you. With this understanding you will create a fresh perspective and achieve a new mastery of your life. I am going to give you some powerful tools that will enable you to discover your inner strengths, solve your problems, and build a happier life.

The method we'll follow is derived from the way I practice psychiatry. While this book is not intended to replace psychotherapy, it is designed to stimulate a similar process of growth and understanding. The book is divided into three sections, each containing a manual with questions and a workbook. In brief, you answer the questions, dictating your responses into a tape recorder, and then play the tape with guidance from the workbook. Each tape is concerned with one of the central issues of personal growth: identity, emotions, and goals.

You can approach this method in two different ways. You can create and work on your tapes or simply read this as you would any book. If you make the tapes, you'll get much more out of it, but you can benefit from it either way. Merely reading the questions thoughtfully is a helpful and illuminating experience. However, I urge you to take the time and effort to make the tapes. You will be rewarded by a deeper understanding and self-acceptance.

A few of the exercises in the workbooks may not apply to you. Reading them may be all you need. Other exercises you will want to repeat several times. Let your own particular needs, interests, and intuition guide you.

The First Step: The Survey Tape

I'd like to gather some general information about you and make a short introductory tape that we will look at more closely later. *You'll need:*

1. A cassette tape recorder, preferably with a hand microphone with an on-off switch so that you don't interrupt your thoughts each time you start or stop the machine.
2. Cassette tapes with one hundred and twenty minutes of recording time each. Use the best tape you can afford. (Cheaper tapes jam and break; that's frustration you don't need.) Keep extra tapes on hand.
3. An 8½-by-11-inch notebook, mostly for the workbooks, but also to record your impressions and insights and to keep a diary of your progress, and a supply of 3-by-5 cards.

4. Finally and most important, time when you can be completely alone and uninterrupted by the doorbell or telephone.

The introductory tape is short. You should complete it in less than an hour, but you should allow three or four hours to dictate each of the longer tapes. You *need not* dictate an entire tape in one sitting.

How to Answer the Questions

Some of the material that follows is explanation, some description, some comment. The questions you are to answer are preceded by a square bullet.

When you come to a series of questions, turn on the tape recorder and read each question aloud before answering. This gives you a chance to record your hesitancy. When you replay the tapes, the silences alone may cause you to remember those elusive alternate answers that would otherwise be lost. After reading the question, keep the tape running and dictate each answer without censoring it as soon as it comes to you. Focus on one question at a time. Be as complete as you feel you need to be.

Many of the questions that follow depend on your very first response for their effectiveness. Be as open and honest as you can. The more open and honest you are, the better this method will work.

Questions that may seem silly, even trivial out of context, have a purpose in the proper perspective. There is some repetition built into the questions. If you've already fully covered a question, skip it. But consider first if the answer in the new context would be different. It might be revealing if it is. Be sure to explain yourself.

If a question does not apply to you (and many may not), you can still respond to it, telling how it struck you.

It is not possible or proper to give you an example of what your tape should sound like without influencing your effort. Your tape should sound as much like you as possible. The length and intensity of each response will differ with each person. The experience you bring to each question, the amount of unfinished business that remains, and your own style of expression will determine your responses.

Some questions appear in groups and are meant to set the mood for as open and full a response as you can give. Other questions are single statements that search for an attitude or a single phrase. Questions that may elicit a long answer in one person will be responded to briefly by another. At the risk of letting you feel a bit on your own, I have carefully avoided guiding you too much.

The tapes must be shaped by the direction of your needs. Feel free to give whatever response comes from within you so long as it is what you truthfully feel. All other considerations are much less important.

Although you are the only witness to much of what has happened to you, some of what you report will be altered to fit a particular view of yourself. Later, we will examine the accuracy of that viewpoint. For the moment, it is best to give your answer as soon as it forms. If you feel you must correct what you have said, do so, but don't go back and erase anything. Remember that you are trying to make a candid record of your life so you can review it and learn from it, even from the way you change your mind. If you can't answer or remember exactly, say what comes into your mind and move on, but always give some response.

Before getting into the heart of this method, I want you to make the brief survey tape. This is to get you used to the process and also for other purposes that will become clear as we go along. In any case it will, I trust, prove to be an exciting and revealing exercise.

Go ahead, get your tape recorder. We're ready to begin.

Some Personal Questions

You should now be alone in a quiet room, comfortable and free from interruption. Close your eyes for a minute and relax.

- What credit did you deserve and not receive?
- What recognition was denied you?

Speak freely. Tell how you felt about it. Say who was to blame and why. Be specific.

- What appreciation is missing in your life now? From whom?
- What would you like others to tell you?
- Why is their approval so important to you?

- Is there something you once said that you'd like to take back?
- What led up to your comment?
- What should you have said?
- What difference would that have made?

- Is there something you once did that you would like to erase as well?

- Is there something you didn't do that you'd like to go back and do?
- If you could, how would you repair your past mistakes? List the important ones.

How often do you think about such questions? If you said "Never," you aren't being totally honest. But if you worry about such things all the time, you haven't come to terms with yourself.

- What were the biggest misunderstandings you've been involved in?
- Who didn't understand what?
- What could have prevented the problem?
- What aggravated it?
- Has the problem been resolved?

I know this is very private, but this is between you and me. And I have to know to be able to help.

- What feelings do you hold in and why?
- What happens to these feelings?
- What sorts of situations make you timid?
- When do you feel like a phony?
- When do you act like someone you're not?
- When are you likely to put on airs or pretend to be more than you are?

- When have you acted insincerely?

I know there are times when you don't tell the truth because you don't want to hurt others' feelings. I don't mean that. I want to know about the times you say things you don't mean to get an advantage, when you flatter or cater to someone, when you deceive for gain.

- Would you have been able to get what you wanted if you had been direct and honest?

- Do you ever find yourself "doing a number"?
- When?

"Doing a number" is a combination of exaggerating your feelings and showing off, usually at the expense of someone else. It's a form of putdown, a kind of criticism. Doing a number says, "I'm great; you're not so hot." Kids are natural targets for parents' numbers and vice versa. Playing sick, crazy, conceited, and bragging are all numbers.

- What are some of the numbers you have done and why?

- What are the most embarrassing things that have happened to you?

Dictate these as soon as they come into your mind. Don't edit them out. If an event comes to mind, I want you to share it with me.

- In each incident, what did people see that you wished they hadn't?

Everyone wants the earth to open up and swallow them when they feel embarrassed. The reason you get embarrassed is that some truth about you is revealed before you're ready to accept it and you wish to hide from it.

- What truth did you see?
- Do the same sorts of things embarrass you now as when you were younger?

There are times when you suddenly see a part of yourself that you wish wasn't there, such as when you overreact and hurt someone you love.

- What have you seen about yourself that you didn't like?
- What allowed you to see it?
- Why couldn't you see it before then?

The truths that cut through your pretenses may feel like wounds at first, but they are also opportunities to grow.

- How did you come to terms with what you discovered?
- Did you hide from it, dread revealing it to others, or accept it?
- Did you use your discontent with yourself as a motivation to change?
- Explain how you dealt with these unflattering realizations.

Finally:

- What sets you off into a bad mood?
- Are you easy to tip over?
- Do you have a choice?
- Do you stay in a bad mood for long?
- How do you get out of it?
- How do you think you appear to other people?

That's all for now. Turn off the recorder, label this cassette "Survey Tape," and put it aside. We'll examine it later, but we have a lot to discuss first.

I think this book can really help you.

2 | How This Method Evolved: The Feeling Cycle

In my psychiatric practice I followed the usual method of helping patients understand and resolve their feelings. My object was to free them from the negative influence of the past and teach them to deal with the events of the present in a more realistic and optimistic way. Because I am an outgoing and expressive person and open in sharing my feelings and thoughts, my therapy came to reflect my own emotional style.

I always heard and saw a great deal in what my patients revealed to me, and my natural response was to share what I understood in a direct fashion as quickly as I understood it. During my psychiatric residency one of my supervisors used to caution, "If only one person in the psychiatrist's office has insight, it'd better be the psychiatrist." He meant that the patient should be allowed to make his own discoveries while the psychiatrist knowingly observed.

I have always objected to overinterpreting and over-analyzing a patient's comments. Basically it is a disservice. It tends to lower spontaneity by making everything seem to have some hidden meaning. Still, I began to see that if I had an understanding that might help, I should not keep it to myself and wait until the patient discovered it. Indeed, the patient might not discover it and I might forget to bring the point up again when, by revealing a simple truth in context, I could alleviate much pain and suffering. Thus I came to believe that the therapist's silence was often an excuse for not knowing the answer or for not trying harder to solve the patient's problems.

And so I became a participating psychotherapist, telling patients what I felt and thought, directly and candidly, as soon as I felt it. I constantly questioned patients and directed their thinking toward new solutions, and I was pleased with the results. Of course, many problems in getting patients to confront themselves remained. I still found myself spending seemingly endless hours in which patients and I worked over the cooling ashes of old emotions, looking for hot spots, and putting ghosts to rest.

In spite of my directness and the considerable effort I expended, I discovered that most of my patients' gains and breakthroughs came, not at my prodding in the office, but in moments of quiet reflection when they were alone. Sometimes insight was triggered by comments made by friends, sometimes by arguments with relatives. Nevertheless, the best therapy took place outside the office.

The best therapy was life itself.

I became convinced that if a person met life honestly and experienced the pain or pleasure of the moment, he would get better. I also believed that with enough exposure to reality, the feelings of the past would eventually be expressed and a person would become free.

To the extent that a person dwells on the feelings of the past, he is living in the past. The emotional debt he accumulates by not expressing these old feelings is paid in the present, distorting reality and causing suffering. The problem is getting patients to empty their storehouse of pain and use their present lives to heal themselves.

To make my therapy as real as possible, I decided to become as open to my patients as I was to my friends. I realized that I would be talking more, that a lot of what I said would be only my impression, and that some of my understanding would be incomplete or intuitive, and therefore much of it might be biased. Still, my patients deserved to understand who I was and what my limitations were. My humanness had to be unguarded so that patients could take any prejudice they discovered in me into account. I moved my office into my home so I would be less of a mystery and so my patients could feel more comfortable. Some of my colleagues warned that in losing my anonymity, I ran the risk of losing my therapeutic distance, my professional point of view, my effectiveness, and, in short, my power.

Fortunately, I found exactly the opposite to be true. As my patients began to see me more as a real person,

I became more comfortable simply being myself. Instead of losing my therapeutic point of view, I discovered that I was less defensive and as a result had less difficulty seeing the patients as themselves. My clarity and effectiveness increased as I became increasingly spontaneous and took more risks.

But while my patients greeted my efforts with enthusiasm, I also noticed that all the old problems of therapy remained pretty much the same.

I turned my attention to the problem of working through feelings, experiencing emotions completely, so the least possible residue remained. From the earliest days of my psychiatric training, expressing feelings had been emphasized as critical. Any psychotherapy that did not concern itself with the expression of emotion was considered an intellectual exercise. While the patient and therapist might go through all the phases of a therapeutic alliance, if the patient did not experience his feelings, it was largely wasted. Understanding without a sense of release and growth is not much of an understanding.

Although expressing feelings was widely conceded to be the pay dirt of psychotherapy, there was no simple guide through the confusing maze of human emotions. Here, in the most critical area of psychotherapy, therapists were mostly on their own. Each therapist's personal experience became the rationale for his belief about the way feelings worked. There wasn't even agreement on which were the basic feelings. Some ideas about feelings were commonly accepted: for example, that depressed people hold in anger and that grief is made easier by crying; but how these feelings are related remained for each therapist to piece together with each patient.

After several years of thinking and writing about the problem, I developed the concept of the Feeling Cycle, linking the emotions in a logical progression. This made it possible for me to treat patients more effectively and with much less guesswork.

Briefly, feelings are either positive or negative. Negative feelings are all derived from pain. Pain in the future is expressed as anxiety. Pain in the present is perceived as hurt or loss and is experienced as sadness. Pain in the past manifests itself as anger. Anger is an active feeling. When it is directed outside, at the force that caused the hurt, it relieves the hurt. When anger is not expressed outwardly, it is directed inward at oneself and is perceived as guilt. When all hurt turns into inner-directed anger, that condition is called depression. There are three main classes of defenses used to deal with these feelings: denial, excuses, and pretenses.

I began to teach the Feeling Cycle to my patients, and it enabled me to enlist their efforts in their own cure. It allowed them to cut through puzzling emotions by themselves. When they felt angry, they knew a hurt was behind it and sought to resolve it. Yet, although the other information I gave them in the office seemed clear at the time, when they got home it was often lost, confused, or distorted. Nonetheless, most of their improvement still seemed to take place outside the office.

The question persisted: How could I enhance the therapy that took place when the patient was on his own? The answer, while apparently simple now, did not occur logically.

I had been treating a man who was overwhelmed with guilt and depression over an affair he'd been having and the disruption of his marriage it had caused.

He was a powerful, willful, and selfish person who, at the same time, had an overblown sense of morality that made him hate himself. His reasoning was faulty. He would condemn himself in one breath and make excuses in the next. Nothing he said seemed honest or genuine, and he would frequently forget what I said to him. He continually needed to be reassured that his reasoning was correct and that he deserved to feel better. In spite of all these negative traits, he was a lovable man and a good father. The problem was to get him to believe this long enough so he might lower his defenses and deal with his feelings realistically. His therapy was exhausting for me; it was repetitive and progress was slow.

One afternoon, after what seemed like a marathon of repeating myself, I decided to turn on my tape recorder and record our session. When my patient asked me to run something by him again, I gently refused and told him to listen to the tape. The problem was not in my speaking but in his hearing. I sent him home with the tape and a great sense of relief. "Let it be *his* problem," I thought to myself as he disappeared across my driveway. It was a revenge worthy of inclusion in Dante's *Inferno,* having to listen to yourself exactly the way you are.

Our next session was nothing less than remarkable. "Do I really sound that weak?" he asked. But sounding defensive was the least of what disturbed him. He realized that most of what I said simply slipped by him and that each time he played the tape he tended to block my words in the same way. This perfectionist was badly shaken. Here, caught for his own study, was proof of his flawed mental makeup. All his life he had prided himself on being clever. He was certain his intellect would never let him down. His feelings, maybe; but he believed his intellect would always reign supreme. Now that was cast in doubt.

I explained how his unexpressed feelings were able to get in the way of his reason and suggested that he listen to the tape to see if he could pinpoint what emotion he was avoiding and how. Over the next few weeks he uncovered a wealth of feelings and their source and finally began to resolve his pain and improve. I continued to tape every third session or so, with no special plan except to help him see what he was missing.

From this case, the idea of taping other sessions began to fascinate me, and I expanded the practice to other patients. It soon became clear that listening to a tape of a session increased the benefit patients derived from it. It became equally clear that when no tape was made, patients tended to forget much more than I'd previously thought. Even unthreatening advice could be repressed if it was related even remotely to an understanding the patient was resisting.

I began to tape more of my sessions. The results were not predictable.

Some patients seized on casual comments I'd made and derived strength from them after playing the tape back.

One woman discoverd a point I'd missed entirely, and it became the turning point in her recovery. Her constant chatter had served to block my perception of her, but this pattern became clear to her after playing her tape.

After hearing how much pain he was feeling while

describing his relationship, one man finally admitted his unhappiness and found the strength to make a change.

As my patients' objectivity in listening increased, so did their understanding. A comment that seemed important during the session was often not nearly as important as the reasoning that led up to it. Some patients played the tape merely to get into a good mood by immersing themselves in my logic. Others repeated my advice until it became part of them. But the most impressive discovery was the critical understanding patients brought to listening to the tapes. The tapes had caught their likeness and fascinated them.

A pattern seemed to be emerging in the way patients reacted to the tapes. First they resisted listening at all. It was too embarrassing to hear themselves sounding so needy, so disorganized, so phony, or so childish. "Is that really me?" was their common sentiment. It was a powerful dose of reality. Previously when I'd tried to tell patients what they sounded like or how they reacted, they denied it or pretended I was exaggerating; now they could not escape the truth.

In listening to the tapes, patients often discovered they really didn't like the way they appeared. While formerly they might have confessed to some trivial flaw like being selfish or greedy, they were now forced to confront a demanding, whiny, complaining self or worse. Some patients stopped listening at this point, claiming it was too painful. Even so, the experience of listening provided them with an undeniable reality and motivated them to change. In seeing themselves as they really were, they began to understand why the world treated them the way it did. They discovered that people acted toward them the same way they reacted to the self they heard captured on the tapes. Listening to the tape was like waking from a dream.

One of my patients, a teacher, seemed to be obsessed with the tape of her first session. She kept playing it, over twenty times, and canceled her next appointment because she didn't feel ready to go on. She felt there was still so much she hadn't heard, so many issues she hadn't grasped. When I saw her for her second session three weeks later, she seemed remarkably improved in insight, mood, and ability to cope.

There is a commonly held notion about the first session of therapy, that it contains all of the issues that will be raised during the entire therapeutic process. And here, right before my eyes, was a patient who set out to work on that first hour until she'd extracted all she could from it. I expected all this information to have overwhelmed her, but at that second meeting she seemed like a person who'd been in therapy for many months, not just one visit. I decided to capitalize on this clearly helpful device even though I was not entirely certain how it worked.

I began to tape all my sessions.

I had always been dissatisfied with the fifty-minute hour. I felt it confined me. Patients often took up excessive time at the beginning of a session to discuss the trivial details of the week. Often, just as I finally reached their feelings, the hour was over. Being only human, subject to the fatigue of seeing many patients in a day and the blurring effect of hearing about so many casts of characters, it was convenient to allow patients to ventilate and then lead them back to the therapeutic issues once I'd regained my bearings. It was easy to pretend this method was effective, but in all honesty it was uneconomical; perhaps only twenty of the fifty minutes could be considered actual therapy by the time all this sorting out was completed. I decided to lengthen my sessions to an hour and a half to increase the time for the therapeutic work.

I was well aware of the "law" that states that work expands to fill the time available to complete it, but playing the tapes of previous sessions kept patients focused. They found it difficult to dodge important issues. They engaged in much less ritual reporting. The tapes made them eager to progress, and so the proportion of fruitful work per session actually increased.

After a while, it became clear that patients needed more than a week to listen to the tapes and absorb the material. I decided to allow patients to make appointments whenever they'd completed listening and were ready to move on. I had them telephone me during the week so I could check on their progress and suggest ways to listen to the tapes. I encouraged them to act as therapist to the person they heard on the tapes: to read the hidden thoughts and feelings; to uncover what was being hidden. I directed them to ask questions of the tapes, such as, "What is being omitted?" "Is this person being dishonest?" "Why is he hiding?"

The hour-and-a-half session now seemed so effective, I extended it to two. My patients were more focused now and, instead of wearing me out, the additional time gave me the room I needed to challenge, confront, and support. There was more to do, more motivation, and the sessions seemed more complete.

Because my own experience had shown me how the discipline of writing clarifies one's understanding and intentions, I instructed patients to keep a notebook and record their responses to the tapes. This not only preserved insights that otherwise might have been lost, it also enhanced their progress in working out their problems. They invented their own questions, relinquished old prejudices, saw flaws in my comments and corrected me, and so we both grew. Each session became eventful because patients had digested the material of the previous session and were ready to move on with an ever-increasing grasp of themselves. The therapy seemed alive, purposeful, and much less repetitive.

Patients now often focused on points that I overlooked in the sessions and made important discoveries I would have missed. I wondered what my old supervisor would have said about the patient routinely solving problems that the doctor was unaware even existed.

The way patients worked on the tapes and the depth of their understanding varied. Patients showed the same patterns in working with the tapes that they did in living. Keeping a notebook made that pattern clear to them. Dealing with the tapes at home extended the process of therapy into my patients' lives.

I have always believed that every therapeutic session should be revealing, helpful, and a step forward. In practice, this goal is often hard to achieve. When patients are forced to fit into a regular schedule, they sometimes have little new to report and feel resentful about coming. The therapeutic effort seems tarnished by a vain struggle to make something significant happen during these periods when nothing much is going on. While purists may argue that these dry periods are an important part of the therapeutic process, I disagree. When the therapist and patient do little but endure each other's uninspired presence and make therapeutic small talk, it is always a waste of time. It may well be that the unexamined life is not worth living, but the unlived life is not worth examining.

I trained at an outpatient clinic where short-term psychotherapy was the major therapeutic model. We saw patients for twelve hours, focusing on specific, time-limited issues, helped solve the pressing problems, and were done. Several of my patients completed therapy in three sessions, one or two in four, and others in six. Based on this experience, I decided to limit my taped therapy to four sessions, each two hours long, spaced at intervals determined by the patient's readiness to move ahead.

For the past six years I have been treating patients according to this method. I have found it possible to make excellent progress over the four to six months it takes for the average patient to complete the four sessions. Within this time, patients are motivated to address themselves to real issues, resolving painful feelings, understanding defenses, and defining goals. The method encourages openness and progress. It's awfully hard to listen to yourself tell lies to a therapist and feel good about yourself. Patients feel a great sense of relief in letting go of what doesn't work, and the tapes have a way of making what doesn't work stand out. The tapes also enhance a sense of personal integrity as patients free themselves from the negative forces that bind them and begin at last to act in their own best interests.

Most of the work is done by the patients, not by me. In learning to discover a new point of view, patients become attracted to their healthy side, rather than dependent on me, and learn to solve their own problems. This confident attitude gradually gives birth to a new sense of freedom. The intensity of the work creates a momentum toward health. The tape method supports the best in patients as much as it validates the worst. Self-esteem rises as the ability to cope improves and optimism and well-being replace a feeling of hopelessness.

During the past few years, I have created different devices for releasing pent-up emotions. I also developed patterns of questions to facilitate working through specific issues in replaying the tapes. These instructions for each replay are designed to lower the patient's defensiveness and increase awareness. As a result the tapes seem alive, for patients continually hear information they had formerly blocked.

Because my own life was full of activities, I developed what I call an Action Board. I wrote the title of each of my projects on a 3-by-5 card and put it on a large bulletin board. Beneath each card I posted the next step necessary to reach each goal. This formed a visual map of my direction and made it easier to control events and reach success. I incorporated this device into therapy as an aid in defining and attaining patients' goals.

One thing is certain. The method works, and any patient who is willing to make an effort at using it gets better.

There are many roads to enlightenment. I do not claim that this method is the only one or that it will inspire everyone to be better, but if you are willing to make an honest effort, this book will guide you toward a more independent, fulfilled, and giving self. The road to personal freedom is paved with responsibility. If you want to be the master of your own destiny, this method is a good way to begin.

3 | How to Use This Book

This method is a means of beginning a therapeutic process within you that leads from dishonesty to truth, from closed to open, and from suffering to peace. It will help you get rid of what doesn't work for you and allow your strengths to emerge.

Although the method is straightforward, your attitude toward the three tapes you are about to create is critical.

If you are open and dictate each tape with a sense of commitment, the material you'll have to work with will be rich and pertinent.

If you are withholding and casual, your tapes will reflect it.

In either case, your tapes will be a study of the way you are and how you solve problems.

Remember, it is far better to read this simply as a book on self-discovery and answer the questions to yourself than it is to toy insincerely with making the tapes. Again, the book is designed to be used either way, but the gains from making the tapes are much further-reaching.

I'm asking for a *sincere* effort from you, a *commitment* to the truth. I'd like you to expose your soul to yourself and capture that act on tape. Give to this effort as much as you can, even if you think the truth is unflattering. The important thing right now is that you decide to answer the questions openly and listen attentively to your tapes. The resulting growth process that will take hold will stay with you for years.

One of the wonderful results of making a commitment like this is that you can borrow strength from it. If you decide to work out your problems, you know that someday you'll feel much better. Knowing that that day is now only a matter of time, you can borrow from your faith in the future, fill the present with hope, and act confidently.

One more point. Don't blame anyone else for the way your life has turned out.

It's mostly your fault.

Don't be put off by that because it's largely true. You played the major role in determining how everything in your life turned out.

That's not necessarily bad. If you can admit this, it can become your greatest strength. If you had the power to make things go wrong, you also have the power to make things go well.

Your life is the logical result of the way you have been. It took everything that happened to you to make you the person you are. Don't lament the past. Don't defend it, either. After all, if you were right all that time, why do you have such problems today?

The first thing you have to do is admit the truth and learn from it. You have a choice. You can do something about your life. If you can assume responsibility for what went wrong, you can take credit for the success you'll have. If you don't, you'll only repeat past mistakes.

You deserve to be happy.

Why put it off any longer?

Let's figure out what happened. Let's do something about it.

4 | Tape I: Who You Are and How You Got That Way

This manual is divided into titled sections. If you wish to take a rest in the dictation, do so between sections.

In giving your answers to these questions, bear in mind the following: (1) Take your time. (2) Try to give several answers to each one. (3) If a question prompts a statement, make it.

You should have your tape recorder and supplies ready. You should now be alone in a quiet room, comfortable and free from interruption. Close your eyes for a minute and relax.

- Describe yourself.
- What kind of person are you?
- What do other people think of you?

- Are they being fair?
- What makes you happy?
- What makes you sad?
- What disappoints you most in your present life?
- What do you worry about?
- Are you happy with your life the way it is?
- What's wrong with your life?
- What's missing that would make you content?
- What are you struggling with at this time?
- If you had three wishes, what would they be?

It's important to discover as much as you can about yourself. You are the creator of your own life, the most important person in your world. If you believe others are responsible for your happiness, that belief is a burden because it is an illusion. It is a point of view that sees you as weak and passive, as incomplete.

You are always complete just as you are. The person who will look up at the fading world from your deathbed in the distant future will be the same person you are now. Between the limits of birth and death you are always the same you.

That doesn't mean you can't grow and change but that the life force that lives within you is always the same. Your job in this lifetime is to free your spirit from the forces that enslave it, to give it room to be. Your purpose is to let the life force have its way with you, enchant your being, and lead you to become what you simply are.

To do this, you must let go of all the unnecessary emotional baggage you've accumulated. Much of what you believe is necessary you've already outgrown. You're only as strong as your belief in yourself.

Your Family and Yourself

Let's look at the family that shaped you.

- What kind of a family were you born into?
- Was it a happy family?
- Were your parents glad you were born or were you some unspoken kind of burden? (After all, very few feelings in this world are pure.)
- Who resented you?
- Did it show?
- How did your parents fit into the community?
- Did that matter to them or did they feel inferior?
- Did it matter to you?
- How did your parents view the world they lived in?
- Were they afraid, discouraged, disappointed, or exhausted?
- Who else lived in your house and what did you have to do with them?

I grew up in a two-family house where my maternal grandparents and aunts lived on the second floor. This meant that I grew up in a home where my mother acted like someone's child part of the time. The little rivalries between the grandchildren and cousins almost amounted to foreign intrigue. Still, the family all fussed over me and had high expectations. Because everyone in that house respected education and learning, I felt I had to do well academically to be loved.

- What were the family attitudes that shaped you?
- Did you accept them or rebel?
- Who was the architect of your family's values?

- Who believed in you?
- What difference did it make?

Every home is both a refuge and a burden. Because parents are human, they are capable of both loving and withholding love. Hopefully there is a balance between the two that makes living with them endurable.

Close your eyes for a moment and think about the house you lived in.

- What are the feelings you get when you remember home?
- Did you get all you needed to grow?
- What was missing?
- What do you still yearn for that you think you should have received as a child?

Your Mother

I want you to tell me about your mother.

- First, what feeling did you just get when I mentioned your mother?
- Was it a good feeling or an unhappy feeling?
- Does thinking about your mother make you feel warm or empty inside?
- Angry or loved?
- Misunderstood, supported, or controlled?
- Describe everything you see and feel as you think about your mother.
- Was your mother motherly? Was she the sort of person who tucked you into bed and made your favorite dishes?
- What did you talk about?
- Did your mother pay attention to you? When?

- Was her concern really about you or about something else?
- Was she frustrated in her own life?
- What would she rather have been doing than mothering you?

Some mothers, to make themselves feel indispensable, intrude inappropriately into all aspects of their children's lives. They secretly believe that being a parent is the only sure thing they have going for them. Such women have never looked within and don't know themselves. They know only that when they feel unnecessary they feel threatened. When parents are unfulfilled, their children are saddled with their unhappiness. They expect their child to repay them for their sacrifice. It's a bad bargain. Neither side ever feels satisfied.

It's hard enough to succeed for yourself. To need to vindicate your parents' suffering only adds guilt to your disappointment should you fail. If a parent watches your every move, you feel smothered. You feel as if you're not living your own life.

It's natural to want to repay your parents for the love and kindness they've shown, but this becomes problematic when the drive to repay stems, not from gratitude, but from a persistent need to please your parents and win their love. It's one thing for a child to spend his time pleasing his parents, but when you grow up you have to fulfill yourself.

- Was your mother one of your supporters? If not, why not?
- Did she see you as yourself or as her child?
- How attached to her did you feel?

- How attached to her do you feel now?
- Trace briefly how your feelings about your mother have changed over the years.
- If you had the power to go back in time and change anything you wanted in your mother's life or personality, what would you have changed years ago?
- What would you change today?
- Why?
- What differences would these changes have made to you?
- Is that difference something you can make up for on your own? How?
- What do you feel you lacked from your mother?
- How did she let you down?
- Did she treat you any differently from the way she treated herself?
- What effect did this have on you?

Everyone's past is full of disappointments. That's meant as a statement of fact, not to depress you. People who hold on to the disappointments of their past tend to become pessimistic. Such people fear they'll always be unhappy. Out of this desperation they make unrealistic demands on others instead of taking care of themselves. They feel sorry for themselves and act pathetic, hoping that someone will take pity and rescue them. Most of us don't want to be bothered by such draining people and reject them, thereby proving their worst fears true.

- How did you get sympathy from your mother?
- Was she an easy touch or did you have to work at it?

- How did you get to her?
- How did you have to act? Childish, sick, weak?
- Do you ever act like that now? When? Does it work? On whom?
- How did your mother's sympathy make you feel?
- Did it help? Were you stronger after she consoled you?
- Was her giving fulfilling?
- Was her love worth the effort she demanded?

There is some pain in every childhood. Weaning from your mother's care is uncomfortable, no matter how giving or saintly she happened to be. Parents are only human and therefore capable of acting in anger and hurting their children. And parents have problems of their own. There are also moments of special vulnerability in childhood when even the most innocent injury at the hands of one's parents can have a negative impact far beyond its intent. Sometimes you hold on to your old hurt because you're afraid of expressing your anger toward your parents. Perhaps you believe their original offense was too trivial and too long ago to make an issue of it today. Sometimes you don't forgive them in order to keep the hurt alive to justify your anger. In any case, negative parental actions can have a lasting effect, shaping your expectations and coloring your responses.

- What childhood hurts are you still holding on to?
- Even if you never knew her, or she abandoned you or died, what presence does your mother have in your daily life and thoughts today?
- If you could even the score between you and her, what would you do or say?
- What stops you from forgiving her?

No child is ever completely ready to be on his own. There is always some longing for home in growing up. The yearning that remains finds expression in every relationship that follows. The way you still need your mother determines your style of giving and receiving.

If mothers were all free in spirit and totally giving, the matter of growing up would be less complicated for everyone. But your mother had a mother, too, and so she had empty spaces to fill as well. Let's try to get a clearer picture of your mother's inner world and its possible effect on you.

- How did your mother and grandmother get along?
- What did your mother discuss with her parents?
- When was your mother free of her family, or did they control her all her life? How did they do that?
- What was your mother's struggle like?
- What were her fears?
- What was her secret desire?
- What did your mother dislike?
- How did all this affect you?
- What could she do or have done that would make you love her more openly?
- What binds you to her now?
- What makes you want to push her away?
- Is she aware of how you feel?
- If not, what feelings do you have as you think of telling her?
- Is there a hesitancy in your last answer? If so, explain it.

The death of parents is hardest for people who still need their parents' approval to feel secure. When your parents' acceptance determines your self-esteem, it's hard to do anything on your own that makes you feel good. Being free and grown up comes only with accepting your parents and yourself as people and letting each be his own self.

I want you to gather your thoughts together and dictate a statement about your mother, filling in any important points we haven't covered. Be honest and direct, covering the areas of affection as well as friction between you. Mention her ambitions, attachments, frustrations, and hopes. Indicate how in touch with reality she was and how much peace of mind she enjoyed. You should end the statement with a comment summarizing your relationship with her, whether you admired or pitied her.

When you're finished gathering your thoughts, sit quietly for a moment and then dictate what you feel.

Your Father

This is a good place to talk about your father.

Again, answer the following questions as freely as you can and as completely as possible. Ready? Try to answer them in one sitting without a break.

■ What was your father like? Describe him.

As your mind searches to answer, pay attention to any change in your feelings. That is the impact your father has on you.

■ Describe the impact you feel.
■ What forces do you feel acting on you?
■ Is the feeling good? Full? Incomplete?
■ Do you ever have this feeling at other times? When?

The way you feel about your father influences the way you see authority. Even if you reject his view completely, the way your father saw the world influences the way you see the world.

- Was your father a happy man?
- Did he feel his life had purpose?
- Where did his strength come from?
- What did your father think was missing in his life?
- What did your father do on his time off?
- Did he have friends? What did they talk about?
- Was he warm? Did he hug you?
- Did he spend time with you? Doing what?
- Were you his favorite?
- Is there any unfinished business between you and your father?
- Is one of you still bearing a grudge? Explain.
- What did your father see as your weak points?
- Was he right?
- How did he point out your faults to you?
- How did that make you feel?
- What did your father think of you?
- How did you disappoint him?
- How did you make him proud of you?
- Did he tell you?
- Was your father in competition with you?
- How did it affect you?
- Did he take the risks he should have taken?
- How did that affect you?
- Dictate your father's favorite rules.
- What was important to him? Did you agree?
- What lessons did he pass along to you?
- How did he enforce these standards and rules?
- Was he fair?

- Did you respect your father? Why?
- How honest was he? How sincere?
- Was there a time when your feelings about your father changed? Explain.
- All in all, did you consider your father a success or a failure?

I want you to pause here and imagine your father as you remember him. Stay with this picture for a moment. Look for details. Open up your eyes and continue.

- Describe everything you can about his appearance.
- How did he look?
- What was he wearing?
- What was his posture?
- What was the expression on his face?
- What probably led up to it?
- How long ago was this recollection?
- What time of day was it?
- What was he doing?
- What does this moment feel like?

Imagine you are now in this scene as your present self.

- What do you want to say to him or do? Dictate these thoughts.
- What are the things you would like to have said to your father but could not? Why couldn't you? Dictate them as well.
- What do you want him to know or accept about you today?

Some fathers seemed to work all the time. The work was often exhausting and as boring as it was thankless.

Conjuring up a picture of father collapsing into his favorite chair after a hard day's work is sometimes all the father you can remember. You feel sorry for him and would do anything to make his struggle easier. Such memories weigh you down. You feel guilty on the one hand and cheated on the other. He may say he's doing all this for you, but what you want most is a father to talk to.

Whatever the reason for your father's struggle, it is partly your loss. Sometimes he had a choice and worked because he liked the work. Sometimes it was the only job available. But whatever he did for you should have been given freely.

- Was your father a family man or did he regret being attached?
- How did he show his feelings?
- How did your father get his way with you?
- How important was his approval?
- How easily did he give it?
- Did you ever win his approval to your complete satisfaction? When?

When a parent feels that his own goals have not been met, he often expects his child to succeed in his place. Children of such a parent have an extra burden to bear. Not only must they find the answer to their own life, but they must come to terms with a disappointed parent who expects to be realized through his children. There is no way a child can ever make up for the opportunities his parents were unable to find. Frustrated parents often have unrealistic expectations of their children, and it's impossible to please them. In such families, the question of what is best for the individual members is never asked. Duty and obligation replace personal freedom, and resentment reigns. Parents who are immensely successful or even famous pose a burden often as great, for with material success often comes arrogance. A feeling of self-importance in the parent fuels the child's drive to rebel, to fail, and to humiliate the parent into acting more real, understanding, or loving.

- How does all this apply to you?

Your Home

I'd like to know more about the house you grew up in. Answer the following briefly but completely.

- What was it like to sit down to dinner?
- What did you do when you were home alone?
- Was yours a happy home?
- Were your friends welcome?
- Were your parents suited to each other?
- Did they get along together, fight, nag, or complain?
- What was it like when one of them lost his/her temper?
- Who drew the limits on your behavior?
- Who fixed the budget, planned vacations?
- Were your parents affectionate?
- Why did your mother marry your father?
- Why did your father marry your mother?
- Did you like one parent better than the other?
- Did either of your parents change plans or career because of marriage or children?
- How did that affect you?
- What kind of marriage did your parents have?

- Would you want a marriage like that?
- When you visit(ed) your parents, what do (did) you feel?
- Is (was) there a pressure, an obligation, an emptiness, a need to prove yourself, or some guilt, a feeling you were bad?
- What's the feeling that being in your parents' presence created in you, as a child and as an adult?

The Influence of Parental Attitudes

Your parents' attitude toward you determined in large part how you came to feel about yourself. This is no new revelation. It is a simple truth, but one you rarely see clearly because the deficiencies in your relationship with your parents create needs in you. These needs live within you as insecurities and cause you to compensate, to seek affection and praise from without. These needs further distort your image of yourself and make you act in ways that are also distorted.

This is only natural. As a child, you learned to see yourself reflected in your parents' opinion. When you finally do grow up, you learn to cherish what you like in yourself and improve what you don't. You learn to accept yourself and stop trying to please others as a way of proving your worth. Being insecure keeps you from accepting other people as they are. You feel you must control other people's reactions since they are how you measure your self-worth.

As a child you felt insecure. You needed to feel loved to feel worthy. Insecure parents make growing up more difficult because they give inconsistently and create confusion. If their child should succeed in spite of them, such parents take credit for it. After all, they reason, it's their child. Success is expected, even required. It's understandable that the child becomes bitter and feels as if he cannot win.

Fortunately, there is another reality beyond your family. You meet other children, other parents and teachers, and you discover the outer world, where, if you are lucky, you find someone who likes you as you are. You learn to be comfortable just by being natural. If you are free enough to pursue your interests, you develop your talents and learn to trust yourself. The seeds of the conflict between parent and child are right here.

When a parent offers praise only for the highest achievement and even then withholds his full endorsement, the child may become a driven adult who is always trying to accomplish more than he can comfortably attain. Instead of feeling worthy, he feels that he's always falling short, that he has no place to call home, that he is never safe.

The goal of childhood is to develop a feeling of self-worth, to feel good simply being yourself, warts and all.

Everyone has imperfections. If your parents used your failings to control you, you may be sensitive about discussing your shortcomings. Or you may flaunt them as an excuse and fail as a way of getting even. But it's too easy to claim that your parents were right after all and that you aren't good enough and so have to accept a lower self as your best. When you sell yourself short and don't commit yourself to getting better, you risk imposing your unfulfilled needs on your own children. In this way, emotional problems are hereditary because they tend to create the same environment in successive generations.

Rebelling against unreasonably demanding parents is healthy and necessary if the child is to carve out an identity of his own. If a child continually lives his life to please his parents, he's in a losing battle.

If you have to do things to win your parents' love, that love is not freely given. If it's not freely given, it cannot be bought at any price. Loving your child starts with loving yourself. If your parents can't love themselves or admit their shortcomings, it's unlikely that they will be able to love and accept you. You'd have to be perfect. And even then they'd find some excuse for holding back.

If your parents are unfulfilled, you cannot accept the burden of their happiness as your responsibility. You are responsible only for finding yourself. If they aren't happy with that, nothing you do will make them happy.

You must accept your parents as they are, shortcomings and all. They didn't do what they did to you out of malice but because they were the way they are. If it isn't up to you to make your parents happy, it's also not up to you to punish them for the way they've been. They're innocent. They are the way they are. You are innocent, too. You are the way you are. If there is any justice in this world, it is that you must spend your life as yourself, reaping the discontent of your cowardice and the satisfaction of your best efforts. It's a fair system, and no one escapes.

You must accept your life the way it is and fulfill yourself without expecting the world to make up for the loving you missed. Only your love for yourself can make up for the past. Finding and being your best is the reward that will make you truly happy.

No one has an easy time growing up. The people who claim that their childhood was without pain either do not remember or have not yet grown up. Children are dependent on others for their support and care. That is their contentment when their needs are met and the source of their pain when they are not. It is the exposure to discomfort that introduces a child to reality. Pain teaches you awareness. By definition, children are incomplete people. They have little experience in coping, and so every threatening event they encounter is unfamiliar as well. Even the most inadequate parents, no matter how cold or preoccupied, feel at least familiar to their child. That familiarity is sometimes the strongest grounds for the child's trust in his parents. It's no wonder that the fear of the unknown has the power to bind us in unfulfilling but familiar relationships later in life.

Your Childhood

Let's take a look at your childhood and see if we can put it into perspective.

- When you think back on your childhood, what images come to mind?
- Are those happy thoughts or troubled memories?
- What was the most frightening thing that happened to you?
- What were you afraid of?
- How did it turn out?
- Has any fear from childhood remained?
- Why have you permitted it?

- What influence did your brothers and sisters have on you?
- Who was the favorite child?
- How did you know?

- Which child was the baby? Which was the substitute parent?
- What do you owe your siblings?
- What do they owe you?
- Were you close?
- Are you now?
- If not, why not?

- What kind of a student were you?
- Did the teachers like you?
- Besides your parents, what other adult took an interest in you?
- What did you learn about yourself from that experience?
- What were the sources of your good feelings?
- Do any of them still exist today?
- Can they be replaced, reactivated, contacted again?

- Did you have many friends?
- What role did you play? Were you the leader, the troublemaker, the sissy, the clown, the scapegoat, the outcast, the brain?
- In what situations do you still play that role?
- How do you feel when you do?
- What were your hobbies?
- What were you good at?
- Are you still doing it? If not, why not?
- What did you get the most praise for?
- Was there something you always wanted to do that you were discouraged from doing?
- Who discouraged you? Why?
- Did you do it anyway? Explain.
- Did you have a secret ambition?
- What happened to it?

- Who did you share your secrets with?

- How did you find out about the facts of life?
- What experimenting did you do with sex?
- What was your reaction to it?
- Did that feeling change? How?
- Did you have a boy or girl friend?
- Were you popular, a wallflower, one of the boys (girls)?
- Were there hesitations about getting close?
- What were they?
- How did you overcome them?

Again, the object of childhood is to learn to feel secure as yourself, but people seldom leave childhood feeling that way. The best you can hope for is to get a good start. Feeling good about yourself requires that you continue to seek out and develop your strength, whatever it may be, however improbable or unexpected. Your strength is where you've been naturally endowed with the most, where you feel best being yourself, where you feel at home with yourself.

The rule of a successful life is to find and lead from your strength. This implies being free to do what you must.

Your Adolescence

Let's take a look at the story of your liberation.

- When did you start to break away from home?
- What were the forces that pulled at you? A sport, a gang of kids, a hobby, a musical instrument? What vehicle did you use to grow away?

- What sorts of things did you do that upset your parents?
- How did they find out and what did they do?
- What did you feel hurt and angry about?
- Did anyone know?
- How did you express it?

- Did you get into trouble? When? Why?
- Looking back on it now, what did it all mean?
- What was your struggle like, your attempt to find yourself, make the team, be one of the gang, discover your sexuality, climb out of poverty? What was your struggle about?
- Did you have people's trust, admiration, scorn, or envy?
- What did others think of you?
- Was that the opinion you wanted them to have?
- What accounted for the difference?

- What were your biggest disappointments?
- Who treated you unfairly?
- Who used you?
- Who misunderstood you when you needed their understanding the most?
- Where did you run for safety?
- What made the biggest difference for good in your life?
- Where did you find the strength to pull through?

Adolescence, that seething cauldron of tumultuous feelings, moment of life's rebellion. Afraid to be oneself. Afraid to be different. Certain you've gone crazy. Positive the whole world's upside down. I never met anyone who wanted to go through adolescence again, but I know many who still have to free themselves from it.

The lesson of adolescence is to be able to do what you like, even if it pleases your parents.

The rebellion eventually comes to rest and the process of risking, of testing your worth in the world, begins. Some people never take those risks. They take the easy path.

Your Work

An easy path is one that you can manage without exposing your real vulnerability. You can hide in a corporation, in graduate school, in a seminary, or in an insane asylum. The whole world's a ward; only the walls change.

You can also find success and personal fulfillment in the same places if they are right for you. Still, it is easy to pretend to be happy in your work when you're not. Because so many people do, few can tell the difference. You may be able to pretend to get by without taking a meaningful risk for years, but you can't really be happy.

- How did you approach finding your place in this world?
- What was your first career setback?
- What did you learn from it?
- Did it discourage you from taking risks? Explain.
- What was your first success?
- What did it prove to you?
- What encouraged you the most in your career?
- Does your work have meaning?
- Does it fulfill you?
- How has your career progressed?

- What were your original plans?
- How did they change?
- Are you happy with your present job?
- If not, why do you stay there?
- Are you doing the work you wanted to do? Why not?

We'll be talking about this part of your life in great detail later on.

Your Love Life

Right now I'd like to focus on the important relationships in your life.

- Years ago, when you imagined the person who'd be right for you, what sort of person did you think of?
- What did that person look like, talk like, and act like?
- How did you imagine that person would make you feel?
- Who were the people you liked, on whom you had crushes?
- With whom did you fall in love?
- Who broke your heart?
- Whose heart did you break?
- Did you marry or live with another person?
- What were you looking for?
- What attracted you to others?
- Did you find it?
- Did you stay in any relationship?
- If so, did you want to leave? Why?
- Are you still yearning for a love you do not have?

- Have you ever found the right person?
- Are you in love now?
- How much does your happiness depend on someone loving you?
- How has that changed over the years?
- What is your home life like now?
- Do you feel at peace when you go home?
- What do you still need to be happy with another person?

The Other Person

This next group of questions is an inventory to evaluate your most important relationship, but it can be used to examine others. For the purpose of this tape, apply your answers to one relationship. Later you may use it to measure others.

- How cooperative is the other person?
- How much help does he/she give you?
- Is it enough?
- What's lacking?
- Does he/she hold back anything?
- Do you understand why?
- How affectionate is this person?
- Do you get what you need or do you still have an unanswered hunger?
- Does the other person understand you, accept you as you are, know the real you?
- How much do you trust him/her?
- Do you feel any longing for closeness even when you are with him/her?
- Can you be open?

- Are you able to be yourself when you're together or do you feel you must keep some part of you in reserve?
- What part?
- Why do you think it won't be accepted?
- How comfortable do you feel in this person's presence?

- Does this other person love you?
- How do you know?
- Do you feel loved when you're with him/her?
- Do you have to work at it?
- Do you feel you have to prove your love or worthiness before receiving love?
- How much does the other person care about you, your feelings, your interests, your dreams?
- How does the other person show this?
- How much attention do you get from the other person?
- Is it enough?
- Can you speak openly to this person?
- Are there any restrictions?
- Does the other person respect you?
- What do you think could be done to make the relationship better?
- Why isn't it being done?

Now go back and answer these same questions from the other person's point of view.

Your major relationship re-creates the world within you. Every person seeks out traits in the other person that reflect his own needs and fill his emptiness. Partners are always growing. For a relationship to be real, it must reflect the changes in the partners and it too must grow. The meaning of the partners to each other changes with their maturity and ability to care for themselves. While you are always alone, a relationship offers you the opportunity to be alone with another. In the best relationships, the individual strivings of each partner are permitted as a natural expression. The only hope you can have in a relationship is that if you both give each other the freedom to become your best, to fail, to grow, to experiment with the life that will eventually make you happy, you have little to fear from the world, for there is nothing that can compete with a relationship that is truly free.

Your Lifestyle

The way you live your life is just as important as what you accomplish. Being happy depends on so many intangible elements. Let's look at your lifestyle.

- Do you like your present lifestyle?
- Does it make you happy?
- Are you living in the place that's best for you?
- What keeps you from moving to where you really want to be?
- Does your work drain or invigorate you?
- Do you feel you will have to retire to get the reward you deserve?
- What would you have to change to have that now?
- What promises do you keep making to yourself?
- What does that mean?
- When you're not working, do you feel worthy?
- What do you expect for your hard work?

- Is there any way those rewards can be built in to your daily life?
- How much time do you spend playing, having fun, entertaining, or just talking with those you love?
- Do you have the time you need?
- How much time do you waste?
- List all the people whose lifestyle you envy. What do they have that you want?
- Are there people earning the same money you are who have a happier, fuller life?
- How do they do it?

The Meaning of Your Life

In a sentence or two, tell me what you think the purpose of your life is.

- If you knew you would die tomorrow, what regrets would you have?
- Is there anything you could do to avoid feeling this way?

Remember that you have to value yourself. You give yourself permission to enjoy your life. No one else can or will. Putting off pleasure is almost never economical in the long run. There should be some part of every day that feels like play to you, that restores you and makes you whole. You should have some play in your daily work as well. The happiest people are people whose work is nurturing and fulfilling, who are enriched by their best efforts and made to feel good by helping others. If you think these are lofty goals applicable to a privileged few, you're deceiving yourself.

There's no reason for you to work as hard as you do and not enjoy yourself.

- ■ Considering everything we've discussed, list ten ways your life could be fuller, happier.

Being a Parent

Becoming a parent almost never happens in time for you to be grown up. It's usually hard to believe you're a parent the first time. From this new perspective your understanding grows, and you begin to see your own parents differently. You realize they were no better prepared to be a parent than you were. You do your best and come face to face with your own limitations, patience, and capacity to give. For many people, becoming a parent is an opportunity to participate in a giving parent-child relationship for the first time. It is possible to grow again through your own giving. When you give freely, you are always the recipient.

Children are the light of our life, our reason for reaching for a better world, our sweetest treasure, our embarrassment and shame, and the recipient and donor of all the love we can give or accept.

You can fail in business or in a career and recover, but when you fail as a parent, it haunts you forever until you make it right.

You can be happy without being a mother or father, but not without having children somewhere in your life. Children are the mortar of the bricks of time. They bind us to the future and make us recall our past. They are most like us and least like us, our reason for being, our only enduring legacy, tomorrow's newspaper, the answer to everything we think unknowable, our heart's proud hope, our kids.

- What kind of job have you done as a parent?
- How have your kids turned out?
- Are you pleased, disappointed?

- What sort of problems did they have?
- Were they similar to the problems you had?
- How did you help?
- How did you make things worse?
- What would you change if you could?

- How do you get along with your kids?
- How affectionate are you with them? And they with you?
- Do they tell you secrets?
- Do you like their friends? Why?

- How different were you as a kid?
- Would you have been one of your child's friends?
- What do your kids think of you?
- What regrets do you have about your children?

- How much do you try to control your kids?
- How closely do you check up on them?
- Do you trust them?
- Do you believe your children will turn out all right?
- What do you worry about with your kids? Why?
- Do you tell them how you feel about them?

- How do they react to your rules, regulations, and standards?
- Are you setting a good example?
- Are you consistent?

■ If they had their choice, would your kids pick you as a parent?

If you are disappointed by your answers, don't be dismayed. You can decide to do better and feel good immediately about trying sincerely from now on. Try to be the parent you would like to have had. Invite your children to tell you how they feel and listen to what they say. Don't correct them or try to justify the way things are. All you need to do is listen to them and understand that if you were in their shoes you'd feel the same way. They'll feel better just talking.

If you don't like what you hear, ask yourself why. How much truth is in their complaints? You can't expect children to be responsible when you don't want to be responsible yourself.

The Story of Your Life

Let's write the story of your life just to see how we understand all of this. Dictate the following statement, filling in the blanks.

■ This is the story of a person who started as_____ .
  Who struggled to overcome_____ .
  Who grew from_____ .
  To_____ .
  And who wants to_____ .

■ Right now, where do you stand in this journey?
■ Is it where you want to be?
■ Are you obligated to others or free to follow your own plans?

■ What is the next thing you should be doing with your life?

■ What stops you?

■ Looking back on your life, what were the most important influences on you today?

■ When you looked ahead years ago, did you suspect you would become what you are today?

■ What prevented you from seeing your future clearly?

■ Are any of those needs still present today?

■ What five things would change your life for the best right now?

■ How much in control of your present life do you feel?

■ What are the biggest problems in your life right now?

■ How different is your present struggle from the one you **had** years ago?

■ Did you give your best effort to make your plans come true?

■ Have you gotten what you deserve?

■ Whose fault is this?

The steps you have just taken toward putting your life in order are a declaration of personhood. You have said, "I am a person with a history and a destiny." You have borne witness to your life and recorded it. You have captured a part of yourself.

No matter how hopeless some of this may feel right now, you should take courage from the fact that you are making an effort to deal with it.

Every life has moments of turmoil. Every life has periods of boredom, moments of depression, times of sadness and concern. These troubled times weather your spirit and shape your character. You come to terms with yourself by accepting your history as what really happened to you. If you don't have to deny any part of yourself, you can truly be free.

A free person is not one without care, but one who knows he is responsible for everything in his life. He knows the important decisions were and are his. He understands his life has been his choice. Instead of taking the easy path to avoid the stress of the moment, he knows he has to decide, in the light of becoming his best, that there are no easy decisions, that he pays for everything.

This is an important step to uncovering your personal truth.

I'm glad you took it.

Tape I: Analytical Workbook

Listening to yourself and commenting objectively on what you hear has great power to change you. Be sure you take all the time you need to complete these exercises. If you hear something you don't like, don't hide from it. Examine it. Decide exactly what it is you don't like about yourself. Admit to yourself why you are the way you are. It's usually pretty obvious. All you have to do is look. That's what this method is all about.

The workbook is divided into six sections. Each section examines a different aspect of your life and requires one run through of the tape. You should allow for at least one day's rest between sections.

You'll need your notebook. Feel free to write down your impressions as you listen. The workbook questions will help you understand the issues that are important to you or difficult to think about. Use them as a point of view. Put down any answers, observations, or discoveries you make. Be as brief or as lengthy as you want.

How Honest Are You?

Divide your notebook page into three columns.

Play the tape, stopping and starting it as the need arises.

As you listen, write down each incorrect statement you hear in the first column. It may be a half-truth, an exaggeration, a minimizing of the truth. Put down any dishonesty you hear. In the middle column, correct your statement and put down what you should have said. In the third column, indicate the reason for your original statement.

Incorrect Statement	Correction	Reason
My father always loved me.	Change "always" to "usually."	It's hard to think bad thoughts about the departed and I always wanted Dad to love me more. I lie about this because I don't want to deal with my disappointment.

This exercise is very important.

Also, if you see places where you consciously omitted something, put those omitted thoughts down.

Remember to listen not only to the words but to the silences on the tape. Try to read the speaker's mind. You can do so quite easily if you try.

If you hear a response you would like to change, write down the change and why you made it.

If you hear yourself saying something that makes no sense, restate it. What was confusing the speaker?

After you've completed listening, examine your notes and write down the answers to these questions:

- Does the speaker exaggerate? Under what circumstances?
- What makes you distort the truth?
- How is your point of view slanted?
- Whom are you protecting? and from what?
- Did you misunderstand any questions or see additional meaning in them? Explain.
- What is your opinion of the speaker? What do you like or dislike about him/her?

When you've finished, examine all the reasons you distort the truth. Try to answer the following:

- Is there a pattern in your distortion of the truth? If so, what is it?
- What are you afraid of facing?
- Speculate on what this avoidance has cost you.

Once again you should use your notebook freely, putting down any insights and fresh understanding. You are embarked on a meaningful journey, but meanings along the way aren't always clear.

Making notes will help you keep track of your progress. The examples of diaries and responses to this method provided below and throughout this book are derived from my practice and represent real people's experiences. These examples reflect how other people work with this method. Notice how many different ways there are to respond and allow your own needs to shape the form of your diary. In these brief excerpts you will see people grappling with their deficiencies, coming to terms with unflattering traits, expressing painful feelings, and letting go of attitudes that no longer work. Each person must find his own way through this, letting in the truth, bit by bit.

Growth often starts with a painful truth.

Write down all your thoughts. It will pay great dividends.

Deborah is a twenty-one-year-old law student with a long history of trying to impress other people. Once she even gave a date a false address in a well-to-do neighborhood and couldn't understand why he stood her up. She was obsessed with success and deaf to criticism, which she dismissed as jealousy.

Deborah's notebook:

I cannot believe what a big phony I sound like. Who was I afraid might listen to the tapes? None of this feels right. This doesn't even seem like my life. My mother's too nice. My father always belittled me. I make him look like an admirer. We weren't that happy . . .

Did I pretend to be happy to cover for an unhappy childhood or was I really happy but never appreciated it? Why do I do that to myself? What am I feeling so sorry about? I lie so much, I con-

*fuse myself. I don't even know what's real any-
more.*

For Deborah, hearing herself distort the truth was a
revelation, and although admitting these faults in her
notebook might not seem significant, it was the first
time she could do so.

What Your Voice Reveals About You

This is a study of the way your voice expresses pressure and stressful emotion.

Play the tape and listen to the voice you hear. Do
you like it? What do you like about it? Tell why you
dislike it. Everyone dislikes the sound of his or her
voice to some extent. It's important that you get used
to it and begin to see it as another way your inner
feelings express themselves.

As you listen, notice how your voice changes.

Put down each change you find by making a chart in
your notebook.

Voice Quality, Volume	Subject Being Discussed	How the Speaker Felt
Shrill, nasal	Not getting into first choice of college	Disappointed—hurt. Trying to make excuses for failure

Be critical. The differences you are trying to measure will be very subtle.

Note also when your voice sounds chokcd up, tight,
constricted; when sentences end up in the air; when
you speak rapidly; and when you hesitate, stutter,
sigh, or trip over your words.

When you hear yourself making a particular sound, try to imitate that sound, noticing the feeling of your tongue in your mouth and the strain in your throat. Is it pleasant to make? How much effort does it take? Note your observations. If you can discover what your throat feels like when you express a particular emotion, you will have an additional way to measure your experience and tell what you're feeling.

- Notice when your voice sounds open and free.
- Notice when it is deeper and resonant.
- How does it sound when you are feeling confident? Authoritative?
- How does it sound when you are exaggerating, omitting the truth, lying, or covering up?

Again, try to imitate each of these sounds or tones of voice as they occur and remember what they feel like.

If you listen closely, you will be able to hear yourself giving yourself away.

- Do you sound like anyone you know? Do you like the resemblance? At what times do you sound more like that person?
- What subjects, emotions, have the greatest impact on the way you sound?
- When do you sound the best to you?

Turn the tape recorder on and, as subtly as you can, make your voice sound tense, then hurt, then angry. Then make it calm. Calmer. Calmer still.

Play it back. Do you convey the intended feeling?

Also practice speaking with authority, humility, and compassion. Play back your tape. Do you convey sincerity?

Real feelings tend to get in the way of false feelings. Voices don't lie, even though speakers' words often do. You can't project genuine tranquillity if you are tense, but you can begin to loosen up by learning to speak calmly. You can learn to feel confident in the same way.

How You Appear

Play the tape and consider the following points, using your notebook as before.

- How much better is the speaker than he says?
- How much worse is the speaker than he's telling?
- How sincere is the speaker?
- When is the speaker being a phony? Why?
- Is the speaker play-acting?
- What is the speaker trying to prove?
- Is the person feeling sorry for himself?
- Does the person complain a lot? Indicate when and about what.
- What does the person say or do that makes him less lovable?
- When does the person appear childish?
- Is the person boring? When?
- Is the person obnoxious? Under what circumstances?
- What is this person afraid of losing?
- How obligated, indebted, beholden, enslaved, does this person seem?
- Does this person sound controlling, rigid, determined to be right, to have his own way, make others appear at fault?
- Would you want to be stranded on a desert island

with this person? What features, traits, would start to get on your nerves?

- What would make you like listening to this person more?
- Who would you want to hear this tape?
- Whom would you want to hide this tape from? Why?

Bear in mind that a realization doesn't have to be momentous to create a positive change in your life.

Harold, a fifty-four-year-old distributor, insulated himself by his stuffy, formal manner. In truth, it covered a deep sense of inferiority. He tried to minimize the negative effect it had on his employees by rationalizing his style as "businesslike." His notes reflect another subtle awakening. Even though the entry is brief, it had a great effect on him.

I sound quite overbearing on the tape. I'm aware that I can be that way at the office, too. I'm just surprised to see I sound like that so often!

Following this realization, Harold began to observe himself as he interacted with others and made a genuine effort to be friendly.

The Forces That Shaped You

The following chart is a dynamic guide to understanding the way the forces of childhood work to shape character. Examine it carefully to see how and where it applies to you. You should realize that most parents are capable of all of these attitudes, and at one time or another you have probably experienced all of the child's tendencies described. Still, try to determine the dominant attitude.

Parental Attitude	Child's Reaction	Triggering Threats	Corrective Goals
Competitive	Difficulty pleasing himself. Depends on praise for self-esteem. Playing the salesman. Impatience, severe anxiety under stress. Wants to bail out under pressure. Tends to doubt his own strong points. Seeks easy short-term goals, quick success, rather than risk true measurement of self.	Any loss of esteem or denial of worth has panic potential; then grasping for straws and unrealistic thinking and planning take the place of action.	To accept that you are good. Your faults and failings make you human, not bad. To believe in yourself and do what's best for you. Trust long-term goals and keep working. Stop looking over your shoulder. Weighing the competition drains and diverts you.
Jealous	Guilt: over success, since each success is seen as hurting the parent. Tendency to flaunt failures in parent's face and to be self-destructive as a way of making parent feel guilty.	Any expression of disappointment or disapproval.	To accept that you and your parent are responsible for your own lives. To fulfill yourself as your birthright without guilt.

Parental Attitude	Child's Reaction	Triggering Threats	Corrective Goals
Manipulative or controlling	Rebellious, resentful, guilty. Persistent feeling of being controlled. Anti-authoritarian, needlessly self-defeating. Since so much has been done to spite the parents, there is a tendency to doubt one's own sincerity and to lose belief in oneself, especially under stress. Inability to compromise without feeling cheated or losing face.	Any form of control or restriction of freedom.	To learn to trust yourself. Not to blame anyone for your faults, even if you can prove it. To accept reasonable limits without feeling enslaved. To let others be free even if doing so permits them to reject you.

| Critical | Self-conscious, tendency to focus on imperfections inwardly, yet avoid dealing with and correcting them, thus not growing and making the criticism a self-fulfilling prophecy. To blame parents for lack of encouragement while secretly believing you're not good enough. To be unnecessarily negative and pessimistic. In the opposite extreme, to need to prove others are wrong. | Any criticism, rejection, or refusal, especially one based on a real shortcoming. | To learn to accept your shortcomings and work on them rather than condemn yourself. To take a positive attitude, face up to your faults, and start doing something about them. To know you are lovable though flawed. To become a just self-critic. |

Parental Attitude	Child's Reaction	Triggering Threats	Corrective Goals
Ungiving, withholding, or selfish	Feelings of unworthiness, neediness, and loneliness persist. Does not feel special. Tendency to act like the overpunished child. Pushes others away. Always on a quest for a giving person, but the feelings of unworthiness intrude in relationships, soiling them. Wallowing in self-pity.	Any withholding of deserved praise or affection. Any failure to get an expected response.	To learn to give to yourself, especially the benefit of the doubt in questions of self-worth. To accept positive feedback and good experiences as the consequence of your deserving them. To realize others' response to you is not the only measure of your self-worth.
Overambitious	Feels constantly in over his head. Believes he must be wonderful to be loved. Even little setbacks cause deep drops in self-esteem. Great	Any failure or disappointment precipitates a panic of overcompensation. Unplanned free time causes agitation.	To accept that you are always worthy. To gain strength and control through planning. To establish ties with your strengths and stay with

	anxiety over being measured. A tendency to disbelieve successes; they feel overinflated. Wide extremes of self-image cause them to distort reality.		work projects and see them through instead of running. To plan rest and vacations into schedule.
Abusive	Feels like he has a chip on his shoulder. Dread of letting out anger, since he fears that would lead to a loss of control and eventual retaliation. Tendency toward guilt and depression and to be punitive, rigid, and abusive. Doesn't feel loved. Distrustful of affection, yet clings to loved ones.	Any injustice, punishment, fear of being shown up as bad. Failure to be appreciated.	To learn that negative feelings aren't a proof of unworthiness. Try to remember you are good even when you are angry. To forgive yourself and others.

Parental Attitude	Child's Reaction	Triggering Threats	Corrective Goals
Smothering or possessive	To avoid closeness, to feel trapped by affection and yet to act in a childish way that invites others to dominate. To confuse control with love.	Being controlled, possessed, and, conversely, being rejected.	To tolerate being alone without seeing it as punishment. To love without possessing. To avoid acting helpless as a weapon. To believe in yourself as complete.
Aloof	Feels that the world is emotionally barren, empty. Hungers for closeness. Exaggerates value of relationships out of desperation, thereby setting self up for disappointment.	Any lack of response from others, failure of others to meet expectations. Making any mistake that gives others grounds to reject you.	To believe you will find what you need in the world just by being yourself. To understand it is your desperateness that holds others at bay.

Play the tape with this chart in mind and see how you fit in. Consider the following as you do.

- Which situations outlined in the chart apply most directly to you?
- Who did you perform for?
- What did you get in return?
- Who were you afraid of?
- Whose opinion did you fear?
- Whose approval did you try to win? How did it work out?
- How giving to other people have you been?
- How self-destructive have you been?
- What were you trying to prove?
- Where did it get you?
- What negative attitudes still stand in your way?
- What can you do to correct them?
- What were the prevailing attitudes in your own family?
- What did each parent want or expect of you?
- Were they successful in getting what they wanted?
- What was your response to each person?
- What goals would help you correct your problem?

Tom, a forty-five-year-old endocrinologist, spent his life reacting to his father rather than acting for himself. He made the following chart in his notebook.

Parent	Attitude & Expectation	My Response	Goals
Dad	1. Wanted me to be perfect.	I rebelled and made fun of his shortcomings.	To accept him as limited and correct my mistakes to make myself happy.
	2. Jealous.	Rubbed his nose in my success.	To realize he couldn't praise me, but he still loved me. My success has to be *my* joy.

Using what we have just examined as background, summarize your dynamic style of responding to people and life in your notebook. Be sure to identify the issues you feel most sensitive about.

Tom's notebook:

> *When I'm criticized I feel exposed, imperfect. So I try to show other people how brilliant I am. Unfortunately, I push others away when I do. I need to accept that I am good even if I'm not perfect. I need to listen to others and learn from their comments instead of fighting the truth.*

Defining the forces that shaped your character is an important step toward freeing yourself.

What Were You Responsible For?

This is a study of how and when you took responsibility for what happened to you throughout your life.

Play the tape again and consider the following questions as you take notes.

- What responsibilities did you avoid when growing up?
- Did you blame other people, circumstances, the times, social pressures, prejudice, or bad timing for your mistakes or failures?
- Do you still blame them? To what extent?
- How did you fix your problems?
- How did you make matters worse?
- What problems did you avoid? Why?
- What obstacles could you have removed but didn't? Why didn't you?

■ What obstacles still block you?
■ How do you feel cheated or shortchanged?

Divide a notebook page into four columns. In the first, list all of the people who injured you, stood in your way, or were to blame for your not doing as well as you wanted. In the second column, next to each name, indicate what each person did. In the third column, list any action you could have taken that might have helped. In the fourth column, put the reason you didn't act.

■ Are any of these people still obstructing you?
■ Why do you permit this to go on?
■ Consider the key decisions or actions you took that made the difference in your life. List these big decisions and, next to each, the source of your courage.
■ Can you still call on these strengths?

If your responses suggest that you were helpless in the face of overwhelming odds, it is likely that your attitude, not others' obstruction, is your biggest obstacle. Review your notes with that in mind, paying close attention to the risks you avoided.

Your success is limited by the amount of responsibility you assume. If you are looking to be better, accepting responsibility is a good place to start.

Writing Your Own Obituary

Allow a few days between the last playing of the tape and this section. Now play the tape and listen to it as if the speaker was not yourself.

I want you to write a speech to be delivered at the funeral of the speaker. As you listen to the tape, take notes to aid you in composing the eulogy. It should be about a page or two long.

Devote one paragraph to summarizing the sort of person the speaker was, what he stood for, what he believed in, and what he was proud of. Was he happy? Fulfilled? Was he loved?

You should cover what he accomplished in his life and career in another paragraph. Tell what he overcame to get where he was on the morning of his death and how high he rose toward his goal.

Tell how he got along with his family and his loved ones, and indicate what his passing means to each of them and mention how they'll carry on without him.

Just before this person expired, he had time to give some final advice. Record his last words for posterity.

Indicate what his life meant to the world at large.

Finally, make a comment or two about what he should have done differently and what he regretted.

Close with one sentence summarizing his life.

Polish this and make it suitable to be read aloud. Post it somewhere you can see it.

Are you satisfied with this account?

Are you happy with the way things have gone so far?

Was this enough of a life to judge this person's potential accurately?

5 | Tape II: The Feeling Tape

You need to be free to do what you want, but something holds you back. That something is the way you feel. Your second tape is concerned with how you feel right now. Its object is to help you understand yourself and to remove indecision, confusion, and doubt.

You are a creature of your feelings. The forces that inhibit you now may have always held you back. Remember, your life is a continuum. You are always the same person. If you do change, it will be in the way you feel, not in who you are. Sometimes the difference between you at your best and you at your worst seems so great you almost appear like two different people. That difference is determined by the way you confront your feelings. You're at your best when you face them honestly and at your worst when you try to avoid them.

Working with this tape will help you define your style of feeling. As you become more aware of yourself, you gain greater control over yourself. I know you may have rarely dealt with your feelings in a direct and open fashion, so I will explain it all, step by step.

The directions are short and simple. If you follow them closely, you will capture a true representation of the emotions that live inside you. The more accurately you record your feelings, the clearer your understanding will become.

You are going to make a record of every feeling you have during the next two weeks. Because negative feelings create most of your problems, they'll receive most of your attention. You'll need to carry a small notebook with you to write down every irritation, anger, hurt, worry, concern, fright, regret, bitterness, jealousy, sadness, and frustration that you experience. You'll put down your joy, pleasure, satisfaction, and contentment as well.

At the end of each day you'll take your notebook and, following the guides provided here, dictate these feelings into your tape recorder. It's important that you dictate the feelings at the end of each day, when they are fresh in your mind. You'll also find it easier to keep up to date with the dictating. In two weeks the tape will be complete and you'll be ready for the workbooks, which will show you some effective methods for dealing with these elusive emotions.

All of this is covered step by step below, and though it may sound like a lot of work, it's really worth it.

Because negative feelings imply discomfort, they seem larger than they are. So if you feel some resistance against doing this work, they arise from your wish to avoid pain. It's only natural to have some vague fear of restlessness in dealing with unpleasant emotions, but if you have patience and follow these easy directions faithfully, you'll develop a new understanding of your emotions and build more self-confidence in dealing with them.

Before you get started, you'll need to know how feelings work. Study the following description of the Feeling Cycle until you are certain you understand it. During the two weeks of this exercise, it's a good idea to read it each morning before you start the day.

The Feeling Cycle

I expect to be injured . . .	*I'm anxious.*
I'm saddened by my boss . . .	*I feel hurt.*
I resent being hurt . . .	*I'm angry.*
Containing my anger hurts me . . .	*I feel guilty.*
My guilt depletes me . . .	*I'm depressed.*

The Feeling Cycle

ANXIETY *Future Hurt*
The expectation of hurt or loss.
It feels like something bad is going to happen.
(*Use* **Anxiety** *to describe feeling worried, agitated, nervous, scared, insecure, uptight, edgy, jittery, uncertain, helpless, fearful, frightened, or having cold feet.*)

HURT *Present Pain*
The experience of loss or injury.
It feels like sadness or depletion.

*(Use **Hurt** to describe feeling injured, beaten, defeated, like a failure, victimized, crushed, overwhelmed, sorrowful, abandoned, cheated, used, discarded, displeased, betrayed, embarrassed, mortified, crestfallen, disappointed, discouraged, frustrated.)*

ANGER   *Past Pain—Expressed*
The outward expression of hurt, recent or remote.
It feels like wanting to hurt someone.
*(Use **Anger** to describe feeling irritated, annoyed, miffed, teed off, furious, enraged, "bummed out," "burned," resentful, or bitter.)*

GUILT   *Past Pain—Unexpressed*
Anger held in and turned against yourself.
It feels like you are bad and deserve punishment.
*(Use **Guilt** to describe feeling like a bad person, unworthy, self-hating, self-blaming, evil, remorseful, ashamed, sorry.)*

DEPRESSION   *Past Pain—Chronically Unexpressed*
Pattern of reacting to all hurt by holding in anger.
This depletes your energy. You feel lifeless.
*(Use **Depression** to describe feeling chronically listless, blue, melancholy, despairing, hopeless.)*

Your Feeling Notebook

Carry your small notebook with you for the next two weeks. Each day write down:

1. Every negative emotion you feel.
2. What caused it.
3. What you did about it.

Indicate any other events that disrupt your day.

Remember to put down your positive feelings as well, everything that made you happy. Write down:

1. What you felt.
2. What caused it.
3. What you did to increase or diminish it.

At the end of each day, using your notebook as a reminder and the following guide as a reference, dictate the day's feelings in order of occurrence.

Guide for Dictating Negative Feelings

Use this guide for recalling the details of each of your negative feelings and expanding on them. Try to recapture on tape the circumstances that led up to each emotion. Don't use the word *upset.* It's too vague. Give details.

1. Catalogue each entry: Date, day of the week, time, place.
2. Identify each feeling as one of the following: anxiety, sadness, hurt, anger, guilt, or depression.
3. Age of the feeling: Old? New? Recent? Recurring?
4. Source of the feeling or circumstances evoking it: an event, a comment, a realization, a memory, another's action, your action or failure to act. Be specific; name names and give particulars, but be brief.
5. Was the feeling (a) expressed: completely, partially, directly, indirectly? To whom? Give de-

tails. Was it (b) denied or withheld: avoided,
blocked? What pressure or stress still remains?
Did it grow or diminish? Was it buried in work or
evaded by escaping? Was it (c) explained away or
misdirected: Taken out on someone else, a pet,
the wall? Did you pick a fight, blame something
or someone? Or (d) did you pretend it didn't matter? Was it manifested as a negative or conde-
scending attitude, a mood of indifference, or acting above it all? Was it converted into a physical
symptom, a headache or stomachache, or acted
out as unusual or inappropriate behavior, or being confused?

6. How long did the feeling last? Does any part still
   remain at the time of dictation? What did you do
   to help resolve it? Could you let it go?
7. Does this episode remind you of anything? Explain what comes to mind.
8. How do you feel about this as you dictate? Do
   you have any discomfort reporting the feeling,
   any embarrassment or need to explain? Do you
   want to push the feeling away or rush this dictation? Do you feel a tightness anywhere?
9. Additional comments.

*The following was written by Joan, a forty-two-year-
old lady who tried for years to minimize the problems between herself and her husband. Just dictating the feelings made her aware of how much she
hurt.*

1. *Sunday night, 11:30, in bed.*
2. *Hurt over Bob demanding sex when all day
   he's refused to talk about* my *hurt. I'd told him*

we needed to see a marriage counselor. He says we're fine and can work it out, but won't talk about anything and then tells me I'm ruining the good times when I bring up my feelings. There's never a right time, according to him.

3. It's an old, old story, and at this point I'm getting sick of it.

4. After acting busy all night and refusing to talk to me, Bob started to get "friendly" in bed and then acted hurt when I told him I didn't feel like having sex, making me the bad guy. I told him that I didn't feel close to him because he didn't want to hear about my feelings. He put down my feelings as unimportant.

5. I told him directly that he hurt me. But he manipulated me into feeling guilty for not having sex. I resented that.

   Later I developed a headache. I guess I was still angry at him and held it in. He went to bed. I couldn't fall asleep. I kept dreaming about . . . can't remember. Got up and dictated this note.

6. I was irritated with him the next morning.

7. Unfortunately, this reminds me of the last ten years of our married life and a bit like my mother and father. (Makes me ashamed to admit this.)

8. I'm still irritated.

9. Why do I put up with this?

This is a long and rich entry, the sort you might dictate on your tape if you were just introducing a problem. Subsequent similar hurts would be more briefly noted. The point of this guide for dictating is to help you pinpoint the sources and the nature of *your discontent. You needn't go into long descriptions each time for the same issue. Just give an indication of the situation, but do note the frequency and location and other important particulars so you can make meaningful observations. If it's important, if it hurts, write it down.*

When this lady examined all of her entries, she got angry at herself and realized her husband was the way he was and would never change. It was up to her to act. Letting him be the resister was just a way of shifting responsibility.

Make your entries as clear and as concise as possible. It will pay off in the end.

Positive Feelings

It's just as important to note the positive, happy feelings in your day. After all, we suffer through our pain because we believe that life is sweet and worth living. It's important to know what makes you feel good and keep the positive in mind.

Positive feelings give you courage by reaffirming what is right. Good comes from good, and positive feelings encourage you to give your best. They bolster your sense of self-worth. Doing something that makes you feel good also makes you feel sane, real, and true. Being aware of what makes you happy can suggest a positive alternative to sitting around feeling sorry for yourself. This guide will help you discover the options open to you.

Guide for Dictating Positive Feelings

At the end of the day, dictate a note for each positive feeling in your notebook, using the following guide.

Number the feelings chronologically in the same sequence as those for your negative feelings so you'll be able to tell how the two groups of feelings relate to each other.

1. Date, day of week, time.
2. Identify the happy feeling: joy, satisfaction, love, relief, etc.
3. What desire or need was fulfilled?
4. Age of the feeling: new, old.
5. Source of the feeling: circumstances, an event, a thought, a memory, a hope, a belief.
6. How was it expressed? Shared with another person? Thanks or appreciation conveyed? Not shared? Why?
7. How long did the feeling last? Why? What intruded upon it?
8. Can you retrieve the good feeling? How?
9. Did you have any interfering negative feelings, attitudes? What was their source?
10. Other comments.

This was dictated by Joan the next day.

1. *Monday, 2:00 P.M.*
2. *Happy, listening to a Luciano Pavarotti recording.*
3. *I felt peaceful, relaxed. Pavarotti is so feeling and soulful. I need more of that in my life.*
4. *I have always loved performers who give to their audience. I have always needed to be given to . . . and to give!*
5. *Pavarotti inspires me.*
6. *Not shared with anyone. This is how I preferred it. It was all my experience.*

7. *Interrupted by the telephone. Person hung up when I answered. Maybe it was Bob checking on me? One of these days I may give him something to check up on.*
8. *Put the record back on the turntable.*
9. *Unfortunately, I started to feel bad that I didn't have someone to share this with. (Am I contradicting myself? Is #6 a lie?) I guess Bob and I never seem to be calm enough together to enjoy these other happier things together. Hmmmm.*

Honestly reported, these entries will give you the perspective you need to think about your problems and perhaps even the motivation to act.

Transcribing

After two weeks of dictating, play the entire tape and transcribe each feeling onto a separate 3-by-5 card following the plan of the guides. There will usually be less than a dozen cards for each day. These are your *Feeling Cards.* Transcribing the tapes onto the cards is essential for the work ahead. Transcribing will provide you with a visual display of your feelings and give you a fresh point of view.

Again, this is a bit of work, but no more work than I expect of my patients.

When you have completed the transcribing, you are ready for the feeling workbooks.

Tape II: Analytical Workbook

SURVEYING YOUR CURRENT FEELINGS

Take your stack of Feeling Cards and arrange them by rows, a day's feelings in each. These cards depict your inner world. Let's see what they reveal.

Play the tape as you look at the cards spread out before you and consider the person represented here. Remember to use your large notebook to summarize your responses and understanding. Think of these exercises as a guide to being this person's therapist:

- What emotions fill this person's life?
- What frightens him?
- What hurts him?
- How angry, guilty, or depressed is he?
- Does this person feel like you?
- Is this the person you want to be?
- How much pleasure is there in this life?
- Is this person happy, fulfilled, at peace, or is this a life of continual stress and conflict?
- How alive does this person seem?
- Is this person facing life or hiding?
- What is your reaction to this person? Do you envy, pity, admire, or resent him?

The following illustrates how the Feeling Cards can make you aware of hidden emotions. It is from the notebook of Charles, a fifty-year-old real estate salesman, who had convinced himself that he was happy while ignoring that he was miserable most of the time. Although he refused to admit his stress, his Feeling Cards shocked him with the truth. He hates his job.

I cannot believe that this person on the cards is me!

I'm unhappy all the time!

I complain about everything.

I'm worried about this sale, that escrow payment, offending this person, putting off that buyer . . . It's endless.

I am full of it!

I always tell people how I love my job, how together I am. It's a cover-up! Look at these cards!

I'm not free and I'm not happy.

I'm laughing as I write this because I had a second upper GI series last week and my doctor still couldn't find any reason for my indigestion. I should send him a copy of my Feeling Tape.

The reason Charles could not convince prospective buyers that a deal was right was that he could not convince himself that he was happy. Doubt begets doubt.

As you listen to your Feeling Tape and examine your Feeling Cards, always be on the lookout for fresh realizations. Seeing the truth is the first step to improving your life.

Overcoming Your Anxiety

We are going to look at your fear. Spread out the Feeling Cards and look at the Anxiety cards. Play the tape. Notice when you are afraid and what you fear. Does any particular fear predominate? What would it take to make you secure? Write down your responses to these questions and ones that follow in your large notebook.

When Do You Feel Anxious?

- Are there times of the day when there seems to be more anxiety than others?
- What is going on then?
- What threatening events occur regularly in your day?
- Does the pattern change on the weekend?
- If so, what accounts for that difference?
- Notice when you are alone and with others. What effect does that have on your anxiety? Is it worse or less? Explain.

Worrying—The Fear of Fear

- Are you imagining danger?
- Can you define the danger more clearly?
- How much of this is the fear of the unknown? How can you know more?
- Is there something you dread discovering?
- What would you do if your worst fears materialized?
- How do you plan to reduce the danger you face?
- What action do you take? Is it effective or just busywork, an obsession?
- How much effort do you waste?
- Is there anything else you could do to prevent or minimize the potential damage?
- Do you fear being unable to cope?
- What gets in the way of your protecting yourself?
- How much of the time do you spend worrying about matters that are beyond your control?
- What would you be doing if you didn't feel anxious?
- Is all this anxiety a cover for something else? It's

easy to say "I'm afraid." It's more difficu...
exactly what you fear.

Coping with Anxiety

The best way to cope with anxiety is to consider it as
an alarm, warning you of potential injury or loss. If
you understand the type of loss that threatens, you're
better able to protect yourself. The following should
help you pinpoint your fears. There are three main
categories of loss.

THE LOSS OF LOVE

This includes:

1. The loss of *self,* of life, of mental or physical
   intactness. You cope with this threat by getting
   out of the way of the danger or by preparing to
   protect yourself. This is the instinct to survive.
2. The loss of *another's love,* affection, support, or
   caring, whether through the loss of that person or
   by that person's withdrawal.
   You cope with this threat by understanding why
   the other person is removing their love, accepting
   their reason as valid to them and admitting whatever role you played in hurting them.
3. The loss of *the belief that you are lovable.* You
   cope with this by accepting your imperfections
   and limitations and by forgiving yourself for being human.

THE LOSS OF CONTROL

The loss of control is the loss of strength, power, or
money, the loss of influence over others, or the loss of
access to someone who has power. People who fear
these things often become manipulative.

Manipulative people are those who wish to be loved on their own terms. They don't want others to be free to reject them. However, the more they manipulate others, the more likely they are to be rejected. When manipulative people are rejected, they try to blame others. To justify their behavior, they accuse others of being bad, of not following their rules or meeting their standards—in short, of not loving them in the way they demand. Manipulative people need to realize that others see their manipulation as a hurtful, unloving act.

Very little in this world can be controlled. Trying to control people with money or power is largely an illusion, and a fleeting one at that. People will tolerate you only until they outgrow needing you. Until then, they will merely resent you. The best way to manage your anxiety over the loss of control is to risk allowing others to be free. Only then will you be able to get close to them; only then will you be able to form intimate relationships based on personal worth, not on coercion. When you discover people can love you for yourself, you'll be less concerned with money, material things, and power.

People who have the love of others have no need to control them. Their *belief* in their lovability is enough. People concerned with control, with manipulation, have difficulty accepting this. Their self-esteem is low, and they dare not risk being measured and rejected without holding on to some retaliatory advantage. The power these people seek is always a compensation for their inability to love themselves.

THE LOSS OF SELF-ESTEEM

The loss of self-esteem is the loss of the feeling of personal worth. A loss of self-esteem often follows a failure to perform up to one's own expectations.

The way to cope with such a loss is to admit it. Realize that you are continually growing, extending your grasp, and therefore are bound to make mistakes. Your failures only measure your weaknesses, not the limits of your strengths. Each failure tells you where you need to improve. If you hide from the loss or pretend it's not important, you won't grow.

What Losses Do You Dread?

Examine your Anxiety cards again in light of this new information.

- What are you most afraid of losing? Love, control, self-esteem?
- How do you cope? Do you face the threat or avoid it?
- What do you *do* to cope? What are your methods?
- Do your methods work or do the same fears keep returning?
- Can you pinpoint anything that triggers your fears or makes them worse?
- When do you have difficulty admitting you're afraid?
- Does something matter more than it should to you?
- Are you so committed to some belief of what is right or what should be that you can't be flexible or discover what is best for you?
- What fear keeps you in your place, imprisons you, or prevents you from taking risks?

- Are you afraid of admitting a truth, accepting a past hurt, admitting your role in an event you regret?
- Do you fear a loss every time a certain memory tries to break through?
- Are you trying to keep the world in a special order to avoid facing an old pain?

The Function of Fear

Why live in dread of the worst happening? Why allow yourself to become paralyzed? Why live at the mercy of others or bank on a capricious fate? Waiting to be rescued not only makes your anxiety worse, it leaves you disappointed and disheartened.

Deep within, you know you must save yourself. Accept that. Do whatever it is you must to be safe. If you want to conquer the danger, you have to allow yourself to feel afraid and let your fear motivate you.

Don't be afraid to be afraid.

It's no sign of strength to act brave when you don't care or when the odds are in your favor. True courage means to act when you're frightened and know just how badly you can be hurt. Admitting your fear of a real threat helps you protect and defend yourself. If you know where and how you're most likely to be attacked, you can direct your forces at the right target.

On the other hand, much of the anxiety people feel results from holding on to fear and not acting. Inaction only makes matters worse. Hiding from a known fear only creates a fear of the unknown. Then your imagination works against you instead of helping you figure out how to save yourself. Ultimately, the concealed fear always leaks out. There is no protection against the mindless worrying that sees danger everywhere.

Such fear weakens your courage and wastes your strength.

Worry is blind faith in the worst possible outcome. Worrying is a form of obsession. It never solves anything, never prepares you for what you worry about. Worry eventually brings on the very thing you dread.

Again, if the threat to you is real, ask what you can do to prevent it and accept the part you cannot change. This may mean feeling some pain, but if you face it, it will pass. Holding on to fear keeps the most painful parts of your life alive.

Feel your fear. Accept it as a signal. If you ignore the message, your fear will keep repeating. The function of fear is to protect you. Look at the danger. Fix it if you can. Face it if you can't. Take your losses and move on.

The following is from the notebook of Clara, a forty-seven-year-old housewife, as she considers her fears. Notice how she begins to develop understanding as she records her thoughts.

> *I have fifteen pages of things I'm afraid of and I haven't finished putting them all down. All these silly fears!*
>
> *I don't like this frightened woman I see before me. She has hidden away from the world . . . in a shell. It's embarrassing!*
>
> *I started to think, "When did this all begin?" And it must've been when Caroline went off to college. That didn't make any sense. If fear is expecting a loss, what was the loss, that I had no one to tell me I was a good mother anymore?*
>
> *This sounds so trite, so clichéd. Everything I've*

done has been for other people. Now I fear no one needs me. I am afraid I have no worth. So I'm constantly worrying about not being useful . . . about not being. I guess I lost my identity when Caroline left. Why did I let this happen?

After completing this entry, Clara became determined to understand herself. When her daughter returned for summer vacation, the anxiety increased. This is a later entry:

I began to feel worse after Caroline returned. Each morning when Caroline got dressed to go to work, I felt as if I would explode. She told me that I should get a job and stop pestering her. I never thought about working. I used to tell everyone that Stan expected me to stay home, but he never said that. I said that! I was afraid to work, afraid to compete in the business world, and so I used anything I could as an excuse to avoid testing myself. When Caroline moved away I lost my best excuse! And when she came home and started working, I looked foolish.

Feeling Your Pain

Now we will confront your pain. We will understand its cause and try to resolve it. But before we do, you need to understand emotional pain in general.

Experiencing pain makes you feel sad. There is no way to insulate yourself entirely from hurt, for we are all heir to pain.

Sometimes pain is the only reality. Children who purposefully bang their heads inflict pain to tell themselves they are real. It's like pinching yourself to see if you are dreaming. Pain protects you. It leads you away from danger, teaches you who is safe and what you can trust. It is a reflection of your needs; for although you recoil from physical pain, you are often drawn repeatedly to the same painful emotional situations without learning your lesson. This results when your defenses rule. Your defenses are fueled by your unfulfilled needs.

The Basic Human Needs

You need to be loved, but you fear being unlovable and so you avoid or deny rejection. As a result, you don't cope with your losses and they tend to recur.

You need to master your body, your mind, and your immediate world, but you fear weakness, impotence, and shame, and so you make excuses for messing up your life. As a result, you don't correct your mistakes and don't get stronger.

You need esteem, but fear giving your best effort lest you fail, and have no way to justify your falling short. Thus you only pretend to try and never do your best work. Your self-doubt increases.

These needs become your excuse for permitting defenses to rule.

Even though your defenses arise from unconscious patterns of avoiding pain, you can still choose how much influence they have, at least for a time. If you avoid your pain, you gain only temporary relief; for eventually when you lower your defenses you must suffer pain anew. Meanwhile, instead of using the pain to motivate change, you only carry it around with you. Concealed pain weighs you down. It taints what is good until nothing in life seems joyous or wonderful. Your suffering embitters you and lowers your self-esteem further. It makes you believe you deserve no better.

You need to *feel your pain as it happens* and believe that it will improve. That's the secret of feeling better. Unfortunately, the same defenses that insulate you from pain partly blind you to the rest of reality. Your occluded vision prevents you from seeing what you could do to help yourself.

So your needs lead you astray.

You fear losing the love you know because you fear discovering it is the only love you are worthy of.

You avoid accepting the blame you deserve because you don't want to look bad and so you look even worse.

You pretend not to care just to save face; you are at a loss, not knowing how to express your pain and comfort your aching heart.

Feeling unworthy creates most of your losses. You suffer *most* when you *expect* to suffer.

THE LOSS OF SELF

The impact of a loss always centers about a feeling of injured self-worth. If you are self-sufficient, you are less likely to be overwhelmed by loss, because no matter how much you may lose, you do not lose yourself. Like young children, people who are dependent upon others live in continual fear of abandonment. The cure for this is to grow into more of a person so that being with yourself doesn't feel like punishment. It's always unwise and often unsafe to depend upon others for your own self-worth.

But unless you're a hermit, you need other people. The extent to which you need others defines your potential for desperation. If you don't find contentment within, you're likely to need others to make you complete. If you make finding another person the object of your search for fulfillment and meaning, you place your destiny in another's hands. Perhaps another person will bring you happiness. Perhaps. But it's far more realistic for you to work on your shortcomings and learn to like yourself.

THE LOSS OF POSSESSIONS

If you need money or power to feel good, you set yourself up to be the hostage of an uncertain economy and you're inclined to confuse financial success with personal significance.

Your significance is in your being, not in your possessions. If you liked yourself, you'd have enough to be happy right now. Your best self cares only to be free. If you're free to express your feelings, you're rich, because you are ruled from within. If you limit your honesty out of fear that telling the truth will cost you, you aren't free to be yourself. What's more, if you dread losing all of the material gains you've made because you believe you are what you possess, you fear losing yourself.

Your highest self *possesses nothing*. Therefore in the end, no matter what you have, you have nothing but this self. If you spend your life acquiring possessions, you only lose perspective. You lose touch with what nurtures you and makes you feel good. And so you need more and more, but it always seems to help less and less.

Everybody wants to be happy. With all of today's uncertainty and confusion, that goal still seems elusive. The secret to being happy is to find and be yourself. Too often, rather than doing what makes you happy, you sacrifice your fulfillment, your peace of mind, and your self-esteem just to be safe.

How can you be safe living a life that lacks meaning?

How can you be safe living a life that does not sustain you?

How can you be safe living a life where all your worldly gains leave you feeling empty?

THE LOSS OF ESTEEM

If you try to be something you're not, you always lose. How can you succeed as anything but yourself? By this point, you should understand that it is the way you deal with your needs that causes most of your hurt.

Your first need is to live an honest life just as you are.

Your goal is to accept yourself as sufficient, to create and fulfill a dream for yourself.

Since you'll make mistakes, you also need to learn the lessons of your failures and grow past your disappointments. For this, it's critical to look at the truth and avoid wasting time wishing that life had turned out differently. If you could settle the pain that naturally occurs in living, there would be no need to suffer.

If you can accept your pain, you can accept yourself.

If you can accept yourself, you can accept others.

The meaning of life depends on the integrity you bring to it. Your needs are an outgrowth of the hurt you haven't dealt with and they make you less honest.

Every unexpressed feeling has the potential for becoming a lie because you incur an emotional debt whenever you try to avoid a feeling.

Every energy seeks to be in balance, and negative feelings are best balanced when they are expressed. If you repress feelings they still seek expression; they intrude wherever and whenever they have a chance. This makes you less free. You feel brittle, oversensitive, and out of control as you blow up over trivial hurts. You don't seem yourself when you are a prisoner of these hidden feelings.

End this confusion. Deal with your feelings as they occur. Only then will you live totally in the present, where you have the most power to influence events.

At first you may experience more pain in facing life directly, but it will be short-lived. When you can say, "This hurts," you identify the source of the problem.

And when you let the pain out, the healing begins.

Techniques for Resolving Your Pain

IDENTIFYING PATTERNS AND PROBLEMS

Let's identify the sources of your pain and see what you can do about them.

Spread out all your Feeling Cards and replay the Feeling Tape. When you come to a hurt, find the card describing it. Listen to your report and stop the tape. Then apply the following questions to each hurt, one at a time.

- What is causing the hurt? A loss of love, control, or self-esteem?
- How does the speaker sound?
- Does the voice reflect the pain it reports?
- How does it differ?
- Is the voice tainted with embarrassment, indifference, or shame?
- Is the speaker bottled up or does he let his feelings out?

- Is there something he needs to tell another person?
- What?
- Why doesn't he say it?
- How would the other person react?
- As you listen to the tape, do you notice any pain that you didn't report?
  Identify it and indicate why it was overlooked.
- Do you still agree with what you wrote on the cards?
- How would you change your report?

When you have finished playing the tape, look at the Hurt cards as a group. Consider the following questions.

- What are the most common sources of pain here?
- How long have they hurt you?
- Notice which hurts repeat. Why do you let them?
- Why don't you defend yourself?
- How would your life change if you removed these hurts?
- Which hurts make the biggest difference?
- Can you see any pattern in the way you deal with pain? Do you deny it, make excuses for it, or pretend you don't hurt?
- What can you do to feel better?

Two Essential Lists

PEOPLE WHO HAVE HURT YOU
Make a list of the people who have hurt you.
Next to each name, indicate what you would like to tell that person.

Put the list where you can see it. If you can't do this because you're afraid of risking exposure, consider why you live in a situation that won't allow you to admit feeling hurt.

YOUR LOSSES AND DISAPPOINTMENTS

Make a list of all the losses and disappointments that are bothering you.

Next to each one, put down what would make each better.

Admitting you are unhappy is the beginning of emotional well-being. If you deny your unhappiness, sadness soon filters through your world. If you make excuses for being unhappy, you isolate yourself from the truth. If you pretend you are happy when you're not, you lose your sense of what is real.

You deal with unhappiness by admitting that your loss is real, feeling your pain, recognizing whatever role you had in causing it, and by accepting what cannot be repaired.

Again, *don't avoid the pain.* Allow yourself to feel the hurt. There is proportion to an honest life. If what you lost was important, your hurt will be deep. If your pain is light, you should question how much the loss really meant to you or consider if you are denying the loss or just pretending it meant less. Should you discover that what you lost really wasn't that important, ask why you believed otherwise.

When people lose all of their belongings in a fire and narrowly escape death, they usually feel happy just to be alive. The true impact of their peril shows them just how little their possessions really meant to them. If you can feel the full depth of your own losses, you'll know what really matters to you. Your strength is always within.

> The following is from the notebook of Marsha, a twenty-eight-year-old woman who spends five days each week working and living away from her husband. She started married life as a weak, dependent woman, but got an education, a good job, and moved up to become a successful manager.

> This feels a bit ridiculous. I continually feel hurt when I'm at home. When I'm away I feel strong, able to handle my department and solve problems. But when I come home, I find myself expecting Howard to take care of me. I don't really want him to, so I reject him and we fight. In some way I feel I have outgrown him, but my expectation to be cared for still lingers.

> What do I want? I have my freedom. I have my own world. I guess I don't feel in love. The truth is, I think the basis of my love for Howard was being taken care of. The hurt I've been avoiding is that I don't think I ever loved him as a man, but only as my protector. I always resented that because it was based on the assumption I was weak, but now that I take care of myself, I question if I really love him. I always feel cheated when I'm at home. It's never what I expect.

> I guess I never felt strong enough to let him love me. And now that I'm strong enough, I discover I really don't care. I think I'm the one who's cheating him.

> Admitting the source of your hurt often removes your need to hide from other truths.

Expressing Your Anger

Hurt and anger are always linked. Although anger is the result of hurt, it sometimes occurs so quickly that the hurt causing it is lost in the heat of the moment. Many people prefer to react with anger than feel hurt because they see being hurt as a sign of vulnerability and therefore weakness.

Expressing your hurt is the best way of coming to terms with anger because it makes your injury the issue. The person who injured you is often unaware of having done so. If you retaliate before making your hurt known, he may perceive your display of anger as unreasonable, confusing, or inappropriate, especially if you have your facts wrong. Then he's likely to see your reaction as hurtful, making you, not him, the villain.

If you don't express your hurt or your anger, you leave yourself open to continued injury and are forced to suffer in secret. Secret anger has a way of making itself known. It's impossible to bury your anger without damaging yourself or the relationship with the person who caused it. Keeping your pain inside requires defensive work. If you deny that your hurt and anger exist, if you make excuses that the other person didn't really mean to injure you, if you pretend that you don't care, you end up wasting your strength by holding your negative feelings inside.

When you withhold your anger, you always make your life more complicated.

First of all, you can't contain your anger completely. If you try, you'll become irritable and feel anxious about losing control. The hidden anger that escapes reveals you more nakedly than being direct ever would. Uncontrolled anger is usually expressed explosively and is apt to be triggered by an event that only approximates the hidden resentment. While the pattern of withholding feelings may have been established in your childhood out of fear of retaliation, any unexpressed anger can create a state of emotional brittleness and make you susceptible to losing your temper.

Past hidden anger seeks release. It tends to attach itself to whatever anger is presently being expressed, so you may find yourself overdoing it when you finally decide to let it out. As a result, you may mistakenly conclude that expressing any anger is wrong. It takes a while to deplete yourself of stored-up anger. Old anger has a tendency to piggyback on new for expression. The way to maintain the right perspective is to keep up to date with all of your emotions.

When you hold anger in, you cease to be your own master.

When your feelings are lost, so is your direction.

I once knew a man who was angry at another man. He would cross the street whenever he saw his adversary coming, calling his avoidance a show of anger, but the man he was angry at never got the message. In time, the man got even more angry and began to take longer, more evasive detours. After a while, the angry man began to resent the other man for causing him this great inconvenience. Finally, the two men met, and when the angry man aired his concerns, the other man revealed that he had never meant any harm and apologized at once. The angry man should have felt some relief, but by that time his angry feelings were self-generating. He had become his own victim.

Being angry can become its own rationale.

Again, the best way of expressing anger is to share

your hurt with the person who injured you in a direct and honest way as soon after the hurt as possible.

It's possible to get the person who injured you to understand the pain you feel and to admit his role in causing it. This is often much easier to say than to do, but the matter can be made simpler if you don't try to make a villain out of the other person. Such blaming will only hurt the other person, make him defensive, and create a conflict of major proportions. It's important to remember that while your anger may feel current, the hurtful event that caused it may be nearly forgotten by the other person. People tend to forget their hurtful actions, not because they're bad, but because they're human. Don't lose patience. Explain yourself. Give others the benefit of the doubt.

If you insist on hurting back, you're likely to be in far worse trouble than before because when you admit your hurt, you reveal your vulnerability. When the other person defends himself, he may attack you where he now knows it will hurt you the most.

If you express yourself openly and the other person receives your feelings without defending against them or making you seem wrong, you'll feel better.

Consider how you contribute to your pain. For example, if you've been hurt by the same people over and over again, it's your fault for allowing them to get so close and for not defending yourself. If you've just become aware of your pain, ask for an attentive audience. Indicate that you have something you must get off your chest and that you need to be heard in order to find peace.

Make *your pain* the issue.

If the other person doesn't care about your feelings, he doesn't care about you. This may be a bitter lesson, but it's one you must come to terms with; otherwise you'll just be hurt again.

Perhaps you feel that the other person isn't worth the effort or isn't able to understand you. If that's so, then why do you let the person into your life? Self-respect starts with the belief that *your feelings are important.* Anyone who hurts your feelings has hurt you and needs to be made aware of it. If they hurt you once, you may reason that they may not have known your vulnerability, but if you make them aware and they hurt you again, your feelings don't matter to them. Then it's up to you to take action. Many people are afraid to make an issue of their feelings because they dread discovering where they stand. Unless you prefer living in a fool's paradise, it's best to know the truth.

Expressing your hurt is standing up for your rights.

Once you express your hurt and anger, tell the other person you feel better and appreciate his listening. You'll feel relief, perhaps a new closeness, and possibly even affection. It's just as important to share your conciliatory feelings as it is to express your hurt.

Telling the other person that you are no longer in pain is the essence of forgiveness.

While some philosophies suggest that forgiveness should be quickly granted in the most charitable way, it is contrary to the dynamics of human feelings to do so. Feelings need to be worked through, resolved so that no residual hurt remains. To forgive an enemy insincerely while maintaining a haughty attitude is a transparent and hostile act that spurns the other person and invalidates your feelings at the same time.

Incidentally, being self-righteously forgiving rather than angry infuriates the other person, for you seem unassailable when you conceal your vulnerability. Such false forgiveness is no act of charity, but a thinly veiled manipulative attempt to bind the other in guilt.

If this is where you are stuck, it's a much better thing to be human about admitting that you were hurt and angry. We all can relate to that.

Identifying Your Anger

Let's examine the sources of your anger and see what sense we can make of them. The object of what follows is to make your understanding more complete and put you in greater control.

Angry feelings are a part of life. You can never avoid them completely, but if you can learn to deal with them naturally, they won't cripple you.

Again, take your Feeling Cards and spread them out. Then play back the Feeling Tape. After you listen to the report of each angry feeling, stop the tape and consider the following questions. Remember to use your notebook to record your responses.

- What are you angry at?
- Have you expressed this anger before? When? Why didn't it resolve the problem?
- Who has hurt you?
- Did you tell him/her? If not, why?
- Will the person let you express your hurt freely or will you have to pay for it?
- Why do you put up with a relationship that restricts you?
- Listen to the voice telling about its anger. Is it expressing all of the feelings the narrator experienced? What part of the feeling is being withheld? Why?
- What does this person fear in expressing himself:

rejection, loss of control, ridicule? How real are these fears? Be specific.

When you've played the tape through, review the Anger cards and consider these points:

- Does one particular source of anger repeat?
- If so, why do you let the hurt continue?
- What keeps you from acting to protect yourself?
- What are you so afraid of losing?
- What would you say or do if you could do exactly what you wanted?
- What would be the consequences? Are you sure?

Look at the relationship between the Hurt and Anger cards. Notice how hurts build and persist when not expressed.

See if you can detect a pattern in the feelings of each day. Could you have done something to break that pattern—indicated your displeasure or shared your hurt?

Ed is a thirty-two-year-old executive in his father's electronics business. In spite of an excellent salary and a good working relationship with his dad, Ed continually feels bitter and resentful and carries a chip on his shoulder. In his notebook he discovered what he'd been angry about.

I must have one hundred Anger cards here. Nearly all directed at my father! I love the man. I know that. But I'm angry at him all the time . . . and for such stupid things!

They embarrass me, these Anger cards. I feel I have outgrown being so angry, and yet here they are before me; Anger over not having my name on my parking space. Anger over not being paid overtime. It's stupid! I'm management. Someday this company will be mine. That's my overtime. So why am I angry at my father?

I'm not angry at my father for all these silly details, but for making me a job offer I couldn't refuse. I never did this well as a photographer. The truth is, I'm angry at myself for selling myself short . . . I was happy before.

My brother Harry does whatever he wants and it's fine, but I have to go into the business. Harry is strong. He doesn't care about the money. I'm weak: That's what I'm really angry at.

I don't have the guts to do what I really want. I'm afraid I won't be able to afford my Corvette or my condo if I'm on my own. Except I never used to work this hard before. I put in twice as many hours now. If I had worked that hard at photography I probably could have succeeded.

Ed's admission of weakness became his source of strength. He rekindled his interest in photography, and his new ability to tolerate self-criticism sparked a period of growth and with it more self-confidence.

Expressing Anger Directly
You need to get your anger out!

A healthy person is open with his feelings and forthright about sharing them. A tiny hurt held in with resentment can grow into a consuming rage. Expressing that pain is your responsibility. Others may be at fault by hurting you, but it's up to you to clear up the emotional debris. Holding anger in, waiting to be hurt again to justify pouncing on others, makes you a villain as well. If your situation constricts you, change it. Use your pain to motivate you. Don't keep pain inside. It will surely destroy you.

Consider all your Hurt and Anger cards as a group.

Before expressing your hurt, assess your role in creating it. The quickest way to alienate others is to blame them for your mistakes. Did you expect too much? Did you misread others? Did you distort the truth? Are you easily hurt? Do you use your feelings as a weapon?

Consider your relationship with the person who hurt you. If there's been a long history of hurt, you should focus on a clearly defined recent incident rather than dredging up the distant past. If your discussion is successful, you'll be encouraged to tackle the older conflicts.

When you decide to share your feelings, try one of the following methods:

1. Arrange a meeting: Choose a place where you both feel comfortable. Express your feelings, beginning with a remark such as "I felt hurt when . . ."
2. Make a telephone call: Be sure the other person is able to speak freely. Be simple and direct. Come right to the point. Be brief.
3. Write a short letter, no longer than a few paragraphs. Offer to discuss the matter further.

However you choose to speak your piece, always leave room for the other person's reactions. You only want the other person to accept your pain and anger. If there's an explanation, hear it. There may be a misunderstanding. You don't want excuses. Excuses are a way to avoid responsibility. The larger truth is that people are usually hurtful when they are selfish or thoughtless.

Be prepared to forgive. If you can't forgive, the relationship dies. If you insist on keeping the upper hand to punish the other person, you're still the captive of your own anger. To be free of anger means you're rid of both hurt and the desire for revenge. If you don't forgive you carry a grudge, aligning sympathizers and dividing friendships. Forgiveness is the key to freedom, but it must come through sharing your pain.

NINE EXERCISES FOR EXPRESSING ANGER INDIRECTLY

Even if it's too threatening to express your anger directly, you still need to get it out. Although the following nine methods may seem removed and a bit hokey, they can be very helpful.

1. Angry Letters Write a letter to each person you are angry with. Begin as follows: "I am angry with you."

List your complaints as completely as possible, but take the time to make them sensible. You want the recipient to understand you, not merely to see you as ranting and raving. Put each letter in its own envelope and place them where you can easily see them. Later, if you feel any additional anger, reread the pertinent letter and add the feeling to it. If you have already made that point, remind yourself that your anger is in the letter, outside you. It's a good idea to use a bright red envelope to visualize your anger at a distance. Keep each letter for a few weeks or as long as you feel relief when you look at it.

After a while dispose of the letter. Take it to a lonely

beach and throw it into the ocean. Burn it with cere-
mony. Bury it in the woods or rip it to shreds on a
mountaintop. Whatever you decide, do something
memorable. It really helps to be able to look back on
the event of riddance.

If after a time you decide to mail the letter, read it
through several times. Consider:

Will the person you're sending it to read it?

Will it cause more harm than good?

Are your points exaggerated? Anger that's been
held in for a while tends to blow things out of proportion.

2. Safe Angry Acts Write the name of the person
you're angry with in large letters on a piece of paper.

Expressing yourself with your hands, tear the paper
into as many pieces as you can. The quicker you tear,
the better.

Burn the scraps, thinking, "You deserve my anger,"
or throw them into the toilet before using it. This may
sound crude, but it works.

Repeat as necessary.

Remind yourself of what you have done whenever
you see this person.

3. Taking Angry Steps Write the person's name on
the sole of your shoe. All day long, remind yourself
that it's there. Take delight in getting rid of the anger
with every scrape and step you take.

4. Acting Out the Anger Close yourself in a room and
scream your worst opinion of this person. It helps to
beat a pillow with your fists at the same time. Don't be
afraid to get worked up. If you find that this makes you
more agitated, try getting even more angry at the pillow and screaming louder and longer, for at least ten or

fifteen minutes. The chances are that the screaming and pounding have opened some old feelings and you have to let more out before you feel better.

Don't be afraid, even if you begin to cry. Letting the anger out won't hurt you.

When you have completed this, sit quietly for ten minutes with your eyes closed, breathing deeply and easily.

Wash your face and hands and go for a walk.

Repeat in a few days if necessary.

5. Gym Exercises Put on a pair of punching bag gloves. Imagine that the punching bag is the object of your anger and let go.

Remind yourself of the anger you are releasing with each punch.

Keep repeating, "This for you."

Finish with an extended flurry of punches that exhausts you.

Say, "It's out. I feel better," when you're done.

6. Partial Contact Pick up the telephone and dial the number of the person you are angry with. When your party answers, push down the button to break the connection and start your tirade, pretending the other person is still on the line. Make sure you keep the button down. Hearing the other person's voice is an excellent stimulus to provoke your hurt and anger and bring it to the surface.

7. Psychodrama Techniques Imagine the person you want to tell off is sitting in an empty chair. Tell him exactly how you feel about what he's done to you. Then sit in the chair and speak as him, giving his argument or lame excuses. Then stand up and discredit him. If you want witnesses, put other chairs around and imagine particular people in each one. Embarrass that person. Mortify him. Go back and forth, playing you and playing him, playing witnesses who agree with you. Tear his reasoning to pieces. (You can have your tape recorder running when you do this or any of the other exercises and play the tape whenever you want a little relief.)

8. Symbolic Menial Tasks Allow your anger to find expression in positive menial tasks that consume your energy. Cleaning the attic, the cellar, a chandelier, or the garage are all excellent examples. The feeling expressed in the work should be one of purification. Boring, repetitious work is an excellent vehicle for expressing feelings. Sorting tiny, multicolored beads into individual piles only to have them recombined at the end of the day has been shown to relieve the guilt and anger of depressed patients in a mental hospital after a few weeks. The ritual of tedious work can do wonders for setting you straight.

Baptize each weed in your garden with the name of the person you are angry with and then weed with a vengeance.

You can invent your own exercise, keeping in mind that you should do something to get your anger out, making sure that you do no harm to another person or to property. Causing damage only invalidates the expression of your anger by creating a feeling of remorse. Driving a car fast is suicidal and endangers perfect strangers, many of whom would gladly sympathize with your cause if they knew you.

9. Ridiculous Imagery Billy, an eleven-year-old boy, was continually the target of his four older brothers' teasing. As older brothers can sometimes be, they were cruel whenever he complained. They called him "Sissy" when he started to cry, bottling him up even more. They knew how to hurt him because, like most of the really treacherous villains in our lives, they lived with him. They knew his faults and weaknesses. Here at home where he was most vulnerable, most in need of love and understanding, he was most betrayed. Worse, he felt love for his brothers and was uncomfortable expressing anger toward them. To hate them would be to admit he was all alone.

I suggested that he imagine his brothers dressed up as large rubber ducks, but with real feathers and webbed feet, and to hear their bullying as mindless quacking and to remind himself when he was teased of how funny they looked. When he tried it, his brothers pondered his inscrutable grin, which I made him promise never to explain, and stopped teasing. I recommend this device very highly.

You are the butt of jokes because you're teasable, because you permit others to tease you. Growing up is knowing that you always have a choice. You need to learn to take a little distance and realize that others are not really bad, but will use whoever lets them. Unless you need attention that badly, you can usually get out of their way. You have better things to do than worry about getting even.

When Others Are Angry with You

You have to let others express their feelings as well. Again, take some distance when they do. Don't react. If you don't deserve all the anger, explain that later, but let them get it out. Be their friend. If you know they're taking something out on you, don't take it personally. If you understand how emotions work, you know you'll have plenty of time to defend yourself later. Stay calm. If their accusations are false, you shouldn't be wounded by them. Remember it's their problem.

Accept the anger of others, but don't ask to be the target.

If you hurt them, don't deny it. Much of their relief will come from your admitting this. If you try to justify your behavior, you are in effect saying that their feelings are less important than yours. If you pretend you didn't mean it, they'll know you're insincere.

You're no different from the rest of us. You usually hurt others on purpose. So reflect on how you might have hurt them. You probably had good reason—your hurt and anger, for example—but now they feel hurt.

Whatever you do, don't retaliate.

Accept their view of the situation. Listen to their arguments. You don't have to agree with them, but don't challenge their reality. Just let it in. If you argue, you can't see what's happening right in front of you.

If you argue, you become part of the same madness.

Accept the accusations, the teasing, and the blaming for what they are.

If you feel remorse, say so. The other person needs to hear it.

If you are sincere, your expression of remorse is a healing act. More than that, it is an example of how you want to be treated. Further still, it is how you will be treated.

Your life is your creation, perhaps not the events of a largely indifferent fate. While we inhabit this earth, each of us is a center of life energy. Taken together we are life, an eternal being unto ourselves. It is the goal for each of us to open ourselves to the expression of this energy. Expressing your hurt and anger will open you and will make it possible for you to find the better way.

Resolving Guilt and Depression

Because guilt is anger that has turned upon itself, at the center of all guilt lies an unresolved hurt. Although it's blocked from direct expression when you feel depressed, some anger usually slips out, hurting others and making you feel even more out of control. You lose confidence and live in dread of exploding. This deeply repressed anger creates dark, retaliatory fantasies, and in time you begin to believe you're evil for being so angry and so you withhold anger even more. A deadly circle.

Soon even minor irritations that you would usually express comfortably throw you off balance. Tiny offenses strike you as severe rebukes. You become self-centered. You take every negative remark personally. You dismiss compliments and resist attempts to cheer you up. Nature itself seems to conspire to mock you. A beautiful spring day seems like a cruel contrast to your dark, angry mood. Nothing in the world is permitted to give you pleasure.

You always have a choice.

You can express your hurt and anger or you can hold it in and feel guilty and depressed. While there is much you can do to feel better, people who feel guilty don't feel deserving of happiness. They deny themselves pleasure and perpetuate the very emptiness they complain about. They withdraw from life, believing they will only hurt others if they get involved. When they do interact, they are so bitter and rejecting that being in their presence feels like punishment.

Relief begins by expressing your hurt.

To resolve your guilt you must let out angry feelings, but if you can feel justified in expressing them, you'll feel even better. Try to remember that your original hurt was real. It's your hidden anger that's been blown out of proportion, making you fearful of proving you're bad if you reveal it.

We are going to look at the Guilt and Depression cards together. These feelings are so closely related that it's possible to think of depression as guilt that won't go away.

There are all degrees of guilt, ranging from momentary regret over a trivial injury to suicidal remorse. You'll usually have no difficulty coming to terms with any feeling of guilt providing you admit your responsibility, even if that means admitting you meant to hurt others. This is critical for healing the pain and becoming free again. If you can't admit your part, you can't mourn, and so you must bear the pain with you. If you can concede your role, you can feel relief.

Examining Your Guilt
Spread out the Feeling Cards and examine the sources of your guilt as you replay the tape. Record your responses in your notebook.

For each feeling of guilt or depression, consider:

- Can you identify any trapped anger?
- How were you hurt?
- Who hurt you?
- Have you told them how you feel?

- Is someone or something preventing you from expressing your anger? Who or what is it?
- Why is that obstacle in your life?
- Why does it have so much power over you?
- Why do you consent to being punished the way you do?
- If you have feelings of shame, what do you regret?

Let me help you here. You probably feel guilty because you believe you hurt someone, did something bad, or were injured yourself but held it inside.

Maybe you feel you should have been a better person and not reacted angrily. Perhaps that's true, but accept that you were the way you were under those circumstances. You weren't your best, but you weren't evil. What should you have done? What could you have done? The worst damage you have done in all this has probably been to yourself—in concealing your pain and turning your anger against yourself.

You don't need to understand everything about your motivation before admitting you were wrong or making amends. Just say you're sorry. If others question why you hurt them, admit you were angry. It doesn't mean you are bad! If you can admit your anger, you can be forgiven.

So now what stands in your way? Your denial that you hurt someone? How is that going to help you? Don't you think the other person already knows?

Perhaps you're afraid someone won't love you if you admit you were angry. That reflects a lack of self-love, and you're not improving the situation by denying your emotions. You can't love yourself if you're full of guilt.

Is it your pride that buys your silence? You don't want to admit you were vulnerable? Or is it some mistaken belief that you are perfect and, therefore, couldn't possibly do anything wrong, much less hurt someone?

Whatever your excuse, it's your albatross. It weighs on you like a secret life you're trying to conceal. Everyone has a secret life. That's why other people's confessions hold such fascination for us. We want to look inside other lives in the hope that ours is no worse.

If you regret what you have done, you probably resent what others have done to you. Perhaps you permit others to control you in order to have someone to blame for your failures. If you have a longing to be free that you never seem able to achieve, or if you secretly think about the success you might have become had circumstances only been different, you're probably not taking responsibility for your actions. You are all your own work, even if you don't claim it. No one else is to blame or gets credit for your success and failure.

You are the way you get through life.

But, I don't know your life. Perhaps others *are* to blame for the pain you suffer. Let's look at these cards again.

- Who hurts you?
- Who makes you angry?
- What are you going to do about it?

No matter how badly others treat you, it's still your fear of protecting yourself, growing up, or going out on your own that keeps you under their thumb. But perhaps I don't understand. Perhaps you are trapped for reasons I can't be aware of. Special reasons. Even so, why should you permit any situation to turn you into a person you don't like? That goes against every instinct to survive, to grow.

Remember that you must allow your pain to lead you away from danger. When something tastes bad, you spit it out. When an object is hot and burns, you drop it. When a situation makes you feel bad, you have to express it or else that bad feeling will become part of you. As I have said before, in time you'll lose your self-respect and become lax in protecting yourself because you'll come to believe that you deserve to suffer. You'll remain trapped in a life you hate just to take away the sting of guilt.

When you withhold your feelings, you're living a false life.

EXERCISES FOR DEALING WITH REMORSE

Using the Guilt and Depression cards as a beginning, make a list of everything you currently regret and tell the contributory role you played in each. Indicate whom you've hurt and how you've hurt them.

Dictate a concise letter to each person on the list, admitting your guilt and asking for forgiveness. Don't be self-indulgent.

If you've hurt yourself, write a letter of apology to your best self, telling how you let yourself down.

Here are some points to serve as a guide in dictating these appeals:

1. Don't say you didn't mean it. You did mean it. Perhaps you overdid it when you expressed a justifiable anger, but you still meant to do it. It's

easy to go too far when you finally release a held-in resentment. Explain that.
2. Admit your sorrow.
3. Speak of the pain you caused the other person.
4. If you mention your hurt, try to keep it in balance. It's the other person you're apologizing to. Share your pain briefly, but don't try to get others to feel sorry for you. If you try to manipulate them by bottling them up, they'll really get angry at you then.
5. Offer to meet with them and talk it over.

When you've finished dictating, transcribe the letters and get them ready to mail, but don't send them yet. Instead, read each letter and consider:

■ What do you hope to get from sending it?
■ Do you sound sincere?
■ Are you sincere?
■ How could it hurt the recipient?
■ How could it aggravate the situation?

Only if you really believe that the letter will make the troubled relationship more open, honest, and free of pain should you mail it.

Self-Destructive Behavior

When analyzing your shame over the damage you do to yourself, consider the real possibility that you only hurt yourself as a way of expressing your anger at someone else. This is typical of children who try to embarrass their parents through failure or by getting into trouble.

People who indulge in self-destructive behavior often plead that they can't help it. The truth is, these people often hurt themselves just to beat other people to the punch. If you make yourself miserable enough, other people won't feel right attacking you. Perhaps debasing yourself keeps your critics at bay, but it does nothing for your self-esteem.

All self-destructive behavior contains both the wish to hurt others and an appeal for pity. It is self-centered behavior, selfish and false. If you are compelled to test the love of others by seeing how much they worry about you, you cause them pain and they know it. They may not say anything at first, but eventually they'll resent you for playing the helpless emotional cripple and for using your self-created distress to control them.

This flirtation with self-destruction only works for a limited time. If other people respect themselves more than you do, it doesn't matter how much you lower yourself. It won't be enough to keep healthy people from getting angry at you for trying to manipulate them. Eventually others will close the door to your room and let you suffer through your negativity without rewarding you with attention until, finally, you decide to be real.

Righting Wrongs

You have the power to make it right again.
Not to work miracles, but to find peace with the truth.
You are only human.
You make mistakes.
Confess your sorrow to those you have injured.
Don't apologize and then deny the apology by making excuses.

If you are innocent, why do you feel guilty?
No one says you are entirely to blame.
You are only to blame for the part you contributed.
That's all you have to admit.
Admit it.
Resolve that you won't do it again.
And share this with those who need to hear it.

GETTING FREE OF PAST EMOTIONS

When you are truly alive, you live in the feelings of the moment. If you are awake to life, you experience pain and pleasure just as they are. But if you continually feel overwhelmed, it's probably not because reality is so intolerable but because each injury in the present brings some previous self-doubt to mind. You feel disheartened in facing your old weaknesses again and dismayed that you haven't really grown. Thus your prejudice against yourself and your doubting attitude turn mild fear into panic.

Your present always contains some expression of your past. Although this suggests that no one is completely free, the larger truth is that you are bound only by the parts of your past for which you're unwilling to assume responsibility.

Only by taking responsibility for what has happened to you can you become free. You don't take the blame for fate, but only for your reaction to it. Maybe you couldn't avoid reality, but how you dealt with it was largely your choice.

In the grand scheme of things, it's unlikely that any single choice you made could have been that critically important. Although people often review their past, saying, "If only I did this" or "If only that happened, things would've been different," this is seldom, if ever, true. Sometimes you exaggerate the importance of a single act, especially when you try to blame your failure on another person or a particular circumstance. When you overestimate the importance of a single choice, you suggest that there is no room for error and that every action brings on an inescapable result. Carried to its extreme, this rigid view denies the possibility of forgiveness and growth, of trying again and succeeding. It inhibits you, making you afraid to take any risk even if you think it will help.

No single choice you've ever made is important by itself. You could have worked out your life a hundred different ways, but at the core you would have been exactly the same. And yet to learn your lessons you still need to take responsibility. It all boils down to this: In order to succeed, you have to give up your excuses for failing.

On the other hand, your pattern of choosing is very important. In fact, you can bring negativity on yourself by your attitude alone. Fear begets fear, anger creates an angry world, and guilt builds its own prison. So in the sense that your attitude controls your choices, you control your own destiny.

Look at it this way: If you sincerely admit you were at least partly to blame for what went wrong, you can be in greater control of your life right now, this instant.

There is as much hope in your life as the blame you can accept.

Acting helpless is the excuse of someone who expects to lose.

You stand at the center of your world. The way you see yourself is unique and difficult to convey to others.

Your life is largely irrelevant to other people. Other people care mostly about themselves, and their needs distort their perception of you. If you avoided taking action because you didn't want to offend others, you've only betrayed yourself.

The real problem is not what others did to you but how you reacted to it. True, they may have been to blame for hurting you the first time, but from then on it was your responsibility to take charge or get out of their way.

You may argue that you were too young to know better, too weak or too frightened, or that the oppression you suffered prevented you from acting the way you wanted. Even if there's some validity to your position, does it mean you must suffer forever?

No matter what wrongs were done to you, none can compare to the damage you do to yourself by believing you are doomed.

You need to protect yourself. This doesn't mean that you can't be a nice person. In fact, it's the people who don't protect themselves who end up as the real villains. If you fail to assert yourself, you become resentful and hold others responsible for keeping you back. You're always looking to get even.

You are the one responsible for becoming your best. No one else has even the vaguest idea of what you're capable of becoming, least of all yourself, when you don't take responsibility. When you don't assert yourself, you're filled with doubts because in failing to be your best, you are always falling short of your expectations. If you haven't really risked anything, you haven't grown or discovered a self that you feel worthy of defending. You come to believe that other people are right when they treat you shabbily and that your ideals and plans are just wishful thinking and not really worth pursuing or protecting.

These negative attitudes toward yourself are your real oppressors.

So, *be* for yourself.

Act for yourself.

It will make all the difference in the world.

The History of Your Feelings

Now that you've analyzed your recent feelings and have a good idea of how you deal with your emotions, it's time to examine how you coped with your feelings throughout your life and see what else you can discover about yourself.

Many people live in boredom, waiting for the right person to make them happy or for some future success to solve their present problems. No other person will ever make it unnecessary for you to be complete. It's always up to you to help yourself. A commitment to yourself gives you the confidence to take risks.

Waiting for help only drains you.

Your life is exactly what you believe it's becoming. It is in the present that you create the future.

Living in This Moment

Because there is only this moment for doing and being, you need to live with the present just as it is, untainted by past feelings. If you dwell on past pain, you'll tend to repeat past mistakes. And since you can't return to the past, you'll feel powerless to alleviate your suffering.

Letting go of the past is the natural way to live. A

life that is lived in the past is meaningless because it has no future.

All being is special. Your specialness is that you are a living container for life. Life is evolving through you.

Life evolves differently in different people. The story of your evolution is told in the history of your feelings. Coming to terms with the feelings of your past is the first step to acting freely in the present.

SOME GENERAL CONSIDERATIONS

Play Tape I. As you listen, consider the following questions. Remember to put down any important responses or insights in your large notebook.

- If your life was difficult, how could you have changed it? Perhaps you were too young to help yourself at first, but listen again. What kept you from acting in your best interests once you began to understand who was hurting you?
- How did you deal with your painful feelings?
- Were you honest in admitting them?
- Did you avoid them, distort them, minimize or exaggerate them?
- Did you become paralyzed by them?
- Did you let other people control you?

Other people manipulate you by working on your weaknesses and fears. As you listen to the tape, see if you can understand the part you played in all this.

Your Fears

- What did you fear as a child, growing up, later on?
- Did your fears materialize?
- If they did, how did you manage?

- Did you worry about any recurring threat?
- Did you ever get over your fear? How did you do it?
- Is there any present fear that reminds you of the way you felt then?
- Who comforted you, and how?
- Did they lie to reassure you?
- Did they treat you like a baby?
- Were you helped or left on your own?
- Were you afraid to express your feelings?
- Did you think your anger would harm others? Who in particular?
- Were you afraid of losing control?
- What would have happened if you'd told others how you really felt? Would anyone have cared? How would they have reacted? Were you afraid of their reaction?
- As you listen to yourself, think of all the times you wanted to say or do something but were afraid. What kept you from expressing yourself?
- Were you afraid of appearing weak, that someone wouldn't like you, or that bringing your fears into the open would make them worse?
- Were you afraid someone would retaliate? Who and how?
- Did you hope the problem would go away?
- Do you still have any of the same concerns about expressing your fears?
- What reasons do you give now?
- How do your present fears compare with those of the past?
- How has your way of dealing with fear changed?
- What accounts for this difference?
- When you look into your past and see a fearful

younger self, what words of consolation and reassurance come to mind? Write down all this advice as if you were speaking to that earlier self. How much of this advice still applies to you today?

Jerry is a twenty-eight-year-old computer salesman who is more afraid of admitting his fear than anything else. His sweaty palms and constant restlessness give him away and make others uncomfortable.

As I listened to the tape today, I realized that all my life I've worried about the worst things that could happen to me . . . As a kid, Dad used to criticize me for the tiniest mistakes. I hated that! I was so worried about striking out that I could never concentrate on hitting the ball, and so I always struck out. That's still going on today. I'm so concerned with the possibility of a customer refusing to give an order that I undermine the sale and try to get out of the office as quickly as possible to avoid being rejected. It's an excellent product, but I've been presenting it like it's defective. I guess down deep I feel I'm defective and that everyone will know if I make a mistake.

This is what's on my mind most of the time, but I can't tell my sales manager when he asks because I'm afraid he'll agree with my fears.

I guess I must trust myself. I've gotten this far. I must have something going for me. If only I could believe that!

I see how I created all my failures. Why can't I take credit for my successes? I think I was angry at Dad for expecting so much of me. It's as if

*when I succeed, he wins, and I'm still trying to
prove he is wrong! I'm really in control of this!*

Sometimes it takes realizing how basically futile
your self-destructiveness is before you can give it
up. Jerry's anxiety came from a fear of being bad
because he saw failing as an expression of anger at
his father. Gradually he realized how flimsy his attempt to blame everything on him was.

The Great Fears

Fear of death and injury makes you timid, afraid to
live, to be bold in following the urging of your heart.

Fear of abandonment, rejection, or betrayal makes
you afraid to be yourself lest you offend. But when
you alter the way you are to suit others, you become
less and only increase the chance of rejection.

You fear the loss of power, influence, or potency
when you doubt your worth or lovability, and so you
try to control others.

Only those who do not believe in themselves fear
the loss of their reputation. A person who does good
work and believes in himself has no concern about
honor. Being truthful in the pursuit of your best is
honor enough.

The fear of the unknown is the lack of belief in the
present.

The History of Your Hurt and Anger

Play Tape I again and consider the following questions.
Take notes in your large notebook.

- How sensitive were you to hurt?
- Did you use hurt to control others?

- Did you blame others?
- Did you feel sorry for yourself?

Feeling sorry for yourself is often an excuse for holding a grudge. Keeping old pain alive is another way to manipulate others. When you fill your life with hating, you tend to diminish good feelings in order to justify staying angry. Did this apply to you?

Look closely at those situations where you used your hurt to control others.

- Who were you trying to control?
- How effective was it?

Remember, manipulation is always a cover for insecurity. You're most likely to twist others when you doubt yourself. You also hold on to pain to punish yourself for the anger you dread expressing and to avoid rejection or looking bad.

Now examine your bitter feelings.

- How angry were you?
- How much of this old anger is still alive?
- How did your anger get in your way? Did it create difficulties in school, on jobs, with friends?
- How moody were you?
- When do you get moody now?
- How did you react to being hurt?
- Did you show your feelings?
- Did you let your feelings smolder within?
- Did you lose control?
- Do you still act the same way when you're hurt now?

You can't find relief until you discover the source of your pain and let it out.

Discovery often comes slowly, even when the problem is obvious. Martin is a thirty-year-old law student who is extremely introverted and sullen, but he tries to appear superior and aloof, above the pain and concerns of us common folk.

I guess I've been angry all my life! But I act as if I am at peace! No one knows the truth, but I'm angry all the time! And yet people act as if they know and avoid me.

I have no girl friend.

No close male friends.

I'm not friendly with the professors in school. I probably would have passed Contract Law if I were friendlier. But then again, I didn't study.

Is all this rejection really my fault?

Maybe I'm angry at God for not making me a genius!

Very interesting!

Maybe I'm just angry at myself for complaining about everyone else and using others' stupidity as an excuse for not working harder. This sounds too simple! Something doesn't make sense here. Maybe people can tell that I'm angry! But how would they know?

By reviewing the tapes over and over again, Martin came to accept that his anger was in fact directed at himself and that if he were ever to succeed, he would have to accept himself, limitations and all, and act real instead of pretend.

How to Get Out of Emotional Debt

As you listen to Tape I, make a list of the people who hurt you.

- What hurt do you feel as you write each name?
- If you no longer hurt, how did you manage to forgive the other person?
- What did you do with that anger?

As mentioned before, wherever you find an old injury that still hurts, you have uncovered an emotional debt and an obligation to free yourself. This old indebtedness throws your present life off course whenever a similar injury occurs. For then the old feeling surges forth and you feel overwhelmed and out of control. You tend to overreact or explode and then end up feeling guilty for acting inappropriately or, worse, you hold in the new feelings, adding to your debt, increasing your burden, and setting up another confidence-shattering incident in the future. This is how people go crazy. Your emotional debt is your Achilles heel, but it's hard to see and sometimes hard to admit when you do see it.

The following letters are extensions of an earlier exercise, but they are very helpful and can relieve a lot of your suffering. They must be written in earnest to be effective.

The Pain Letters

1. Write a letter to each person who has hurt you where you still feel pain in recalling the hurt. Describe in detail and in language rich in emotion: how you were hurt, how angry you felt, how you suffered, and what you feel about the other per-

son. Take them through the events again. Let your feelings flow into the letter.

2. If you contributed to the situation, admit your culpability.

3. If you can accept that the people who hurt you did so not because they were bad but because they, like you, were only human and did the best they could, you can forgive them. This doesn't mean that some people aren't bad. Some are. Expressing anger to someone you love is what's difficult because you're afraid of losing their love. But how much is such love worth if the price you must pay to keep it is to destroy yourself by withholding anger the other won't accept?

4. Again, carefully correct the letters and get them ready to mail.

5. As before, keep the letters where you can see them, making sure no one will accidentally mail them. Remind yourself that the feeling is now out of you. This may sound contrived, but it works if you permit yourself to be free in expressing your feelings in the letters. It's even possible to direct anger at people who have died and get it out effectively in the same way. When you can think about the person without any more hurt or anger, you can destroy the letter. Remember, a good plan is to destroy the letters one by one in a memorable way, reminding yourself of the contents of each one as you do.

You may also use any of the indirect methods to let out hurt and anger that were suggested earlier in this workbook. Whatever lightens your burden is good for you. Trust your feeling of relief. Allow yourself to feel any release of pressure. It's important not to hold back expressing your feelings even if you feel silly doing so.

All of this focus on pain is to help you empty your reservoirs of sorrow so you will be able to feel joy. Some sorrows will never resolve completely. Some losses are so terrible that they seem like a lifetime burden. Still, if you permit the pain to reach you whenever it wells up within and permit your tears to flow, time will do the rest. Again, give in to your feelings of relief, no matter how small or fleeting. That is always the right direction to follow.

Seeking Forgiveness

As you look back on your life, it must be clear to you that you were responsible for much of what went wrong. You may disagree, but you have to be an accomplice in much of the wrongdoing against you. Even if it was only putting up with being abused, it is important now to admit how you contributed to your problems.

You weren't entirely to blame, but you were human and made mistakes. If you can learn from your errors, you can forgive yourself. You forgive yourself by not repeating your mistakes.

When you blame others, you overreact to being hurt. Others aren't sympathetic. They see you as self-indulgent and manipulative and resent being blamed, especially when they can see how you bring your problems on yourself.

Your Petition

Replay Tape I and this time consider everything you did that was hurtful to others. If you have difficulty thinking about this, it's probably because you don't feel forgiven.

The exercise that follows will help remove this burden from you.

Make a list of the people you regret hurting. Next to each name indicate what you did; tell if you still feel badly about it and why.

Perhaps you have difficulty admitting that you hurt others because you meant no harm, but there were times when you felt hurt and angry and did mean to hurt back. More often you hurt others with all the best intentions.

If you feel remorseful, making amends to the people you hurt will help to relieve your guilt.

If someone hurt you, what would you like to tell them?

Put those same thoughts in a letter to each person on your list. They need to know how sorry you feel.

Also admit whatever you did that hurt them.

Accept whatever blame you deserve.

Ask them to forgive you.

Resolve never to do it again and forgive yourself.

Be brief, to the point, and, above all, be sincere. Your object should be to make the other person feel better, not to re-create a painful situation for them just for the purpose of freeing yourself.

If you wish, you can mail these letters. If the offense occurred years ago, the person may no longer be aware of what actually happened or may have forgotten the details. In any case, your letter will be a surprise, probably a pleasant one. Or, instead of mailing the letter, you may use it as a guide for a face-to-face meeting.

If the other person is no longer alive, writing the letter will still be effective. Sometimes a gravesite reading of such a letter will help relieve guilt. It sounds macabre, but it works very well. Remember, the feeling is alive even if the person isn't.

Guide to a Graveside Visit

Call out the name of the person and add, "I want you to hear my words. I come to beg forgiveness."

Read your letter.

Summarize your message. For example, "I'm sorry I hurt you. I love you and I know you love me. I want the good feelings of your spirit to be with me always. Therefore, I forgive you everything large and small and know that you forgive me."

There may only be one person in your life to whom this exercise applies, but if someone comes to mind, your heart is bidding you to make the visit.

Reparations

Another way of undoing your guilt is to express your remorse to whomever you hurt and offer to do some kind of reparative work, some symbolic act that will help restore the sense of good intention between you. This may involve using a day on the weekend to clean out someone's garage.

Penance

The effectiveness of doing penance has stood the test of time, and its effectiveness in relieving feelings of guilt and depression cannot be overestimated. Anyone who has ever observed how patients on the back wards of a mental hospital cope with the pain of depression by performing the most menial tasks, such as cleaning toilets on their hands and knees, can attest to this.

Sometimes people get relief by abstaining from pleasure or by punishing themselves. This kind of behavior tends to be self-centered, self-indulgent, socially removed, and not especially effective. It flaunts your self-flagellation far more than it actually succeeds in making amends. Its shock value sometimes has the effect of being a hurtful act of its own. You can overdo this sort of thing and deceive yourself into believing you've made amends, but if you haven't admitted your responsibility in injuring the other person, you might as well not have denied yourself.

The kind of penance that has the best chance of relieving guilt is not merely punishment, which in a larger sense is only adding more negativity to the world, but is behavior that has some social good as its goal. If the penance is properly designed, it will also free you to be good to yourself.

Contrary to what you may believe because of your guilt, the person you've hurt doesn't want you to suffer but to see the error of your ways and change.

People commonly use words to soften their guilt, so merely saying "I'm sorry" may not be enough to make your situation better. Doing physical work or donating your services to some deserving person or cause in the name of releasing you from your old guilt works best, especially when the person you've hurt is dead or when the injurious act you committed was truly damaging. If you choose to do this, do so with a sense of total commitment. Dedicate your work to settling your emotional account. The work you choose should not be done at your convenience. It should not be particularly pleasant. It should only be necessary and helpful. The greater the difficulty involved in your sacrifice, the more relief you're likely to experience.

The most effective penance is relevant to the injury and makes symbolic amends. If you are sincere and your act of repair meaningful, you will find relief. Some penance should be a particular corrective act. Some penance should last for a week, some for a month, others for years. Sometimes it is necessary for penance to continue for your lifetime, not necessarily in sorrow or in shame, but in some worthwhile positive dedication that serves as daily proof of your sincerity.

The way to heal guilt is always through giving to others. Your best gift is always of yourself.

The Meaning of Your Life

Your life means precisely what you do with it—no more, no less. The works you leave behind, the acts you perform whether or not you receive recognition for them, are your monument. It makes little difference why you did what you did. In the end it matters only that *you did it.*

Some people serve as links in a biological chain by transmitting life from one generation to the next. Some uphold tradition and values. Some inspire; others follow and validate their teacher. So meaning can come from giving life, sustaining life, creating wisdom, or accepting a teaching.

Each person is a part of life.

Each life is a world of its own.

Because there is slack in the universe, one can reason that no single life can be that important. Still, who could deny the importance of a single existence as a link in the chain of life?

If you believe that everything you do can be achieved by others, that you are only a number, your life still has meaning. If all the lives that supposedly have as little meaning as you claim for yours didn't exist, who would do the work of the world?

How could the grandeur of the world exist without the workers? For whom is all the spectacle performed if not for the likes of you? Your awareness justifies your existence. How much of life, but for your awareness, would be unknown? How much of the world is held within you? Who will hold the substructure of the world together, sow the seed, applaud the singer, dance the dance, if not you?

Your life is more important than you think.

Consider how the lives of others would have been altered if you had never been.

Who wouldn't be here?

How much suffering did you relieve?

What work did you accomplish that would not have been done by someone else?

The world of which you are the center is held together by your perceptions, your needs, your values, and, ultimately, your feelings. Your feelings center you and organize a world around you. Your feelings are the expression of your life energy.

If you have great skill in expressing yourself, you can change the larger world. Consider the lives of the great artists, inventors, thinkers. Their personal struggle found expression in their art, and their art in turn shaped the world that came after them. Except for nature, everything you see around you is the creation of some person expressing himself. Altogether, these creative expressions are our world. The good and the bad are all our own doing. We take our inner struggles, resolve them creatively or destructively, and share the results. Those are the dynamics of life.

Look at the way you share your inner world. Are you an emotional recluse? Are you open? Are you guarded, afraid to be seen as yourself because you feel that you aren't good enough? Until you accept yourself, you cannot make your greatest contribution. You cannot share your best.

Your life has meaning:

If you are a witness to your own truth and share it.

If you help another person discover himself.

If you relieve suffering.

If you give people diversion from their toil so that they are refreshed in their efforts.

If you survive to tell your story.

If you survive to tell someone else's story.

If you are a performer.

If you are a member of the audience.

The meaning of your life is in sharing your unique point of view.

The life that is not shared might as well not be lived.

Understanding Your Defenses

Defenses limit your participation in life.

No one's life is free from defenses. Still, your goals always remain the same: to become your best, triumph over your weaknesses, grow more honest and confident, and learn to trust yourself so you don't fear the truth. Your intention is to live the best life you can. Self-acceptance and self-love are correct attitudes. Believing in this ever-evolving best self is your strength and courage.

Your life is your moment of truth.

Your defenses are the blind spots in your struggle.

Defenses inhibit both your awareness and the expression of your feelings. If you shared your old feelings and expressed the new as they occurred, very few of the dreadful results you fear would happen. Indeed, you might surprise people if you brought your emotions up to date. Others might not like what you had to say, but they'd respect you for being direct. Once the shock wore off, they might even get used to it. In any case, you'd feel better.

Eventually, if you kept current with your feelings and didn't hold back, your openness would make life easier. That's not to say you'd never be troubled again, but rather that you'd deal with your feelings as they occurred in their proper context and have done with them. When you try to contain your dark feelings, you only undermine your self-worth and invite further injury. Your happiness and your self-love depend on expressing your dark emotions as freely as your positive ones.

If you love yourself, you have no enemies.

Your hatred of others comes largely from your disappointment with yourself. You resent people who make you aware of the weaknesses you cannot accept. When you don't accept yourself, you look outside for reasons you're not what you want to be. This misdirection of blame consumes you. While you secretly know you should improve, you can't seem to get anything accomplished. There's so much frustration and so many people to blame that you don't have time to examine yourself.

When you don't express your feelings, a portion of your strength is diverted to blocking and repressing them. As additional feelings are blocked, you are further depleted. Although these feelings go underground, they do not disappear. In fact, because they operate outside your awareness and thus control, they exert their influence far more destructively than they would if you dealt with them directly.

Your unexpressed feelings make you needy; they lead you to form desperate alliances, to make destructive choices. So it is that when you bury hurt and anger they eventually turn on you and make you feel unworthy, leading you into punitive relationships or to failure.

The purpose of defenses is to protect you from becoming overwhelmed by pain. They are designed to keep you functioning under stress. They buy time to assess danger and figure out what to do about it. Eventually you're supposed to lower your defenses and get to work to fix the problem.

Your defensive pattern is the key to understanding how you react to stress. If you are open, you experience your painful feelings pretty much as they are. Being open comes from having confidence in your ability to cope. Problems occur when a defense becomes rigid and compromises your ability to act freely, when you employ your defenses, not by choice, but as a habit built into your character. Like all habits, using a particular defense began when it seemed useful in context and appropriate in amount. And since defenses have long-established roots in the past, they also have a prefabricated, predictable quality that gets in your way.

You can attain greater mastery over your defenses by becoming aware of how they work, seeing how and when you depend on them, and by learning to solve the problem they obscure. That problem always has something to do with your feelings.

The exercises in this section will be challenging because they focus on uncovering what you prefer not to know, not to see: the pain behind your defenses. But before you continue, it's important to understand how defenses work. There are three broad classes of defenses: denial, excuses, and pretenses.

Denial

Denial is the insistence that something that exists does not exist.

You can get away with saying "No" to reality for a moment, such as on hearing bad news, or you can maintain a false belief for years and insist that the bad news never occurred. You can also deny your weakness by identifying with someone stronger and acting as if you were that person, a common practice in childhood.

As you relinquish your denial, your experience of pain increases until it is accepted. It's common on hearing of the death of someone you love to use a great deal of denial. You say "No." You just can't believe it. The mourning process gradually removes the denial that separates you from your loss. Mourning rituals confront mourners with parts of reality that are increasingly difficult to deny until, finally, the full impact of the loss can be felt.

Denial is used to defend against a loss of love, a loss of self, or the loss of another.

Excuses

Excuses include all of the intellectual processes that stand in the way of feeling, including rationalizing, blaming, and explaining away both the hurt done to you and the hurt you do to others. In the case of hurting others, you excuse yourself so you don't have to feel guilty. You reason that you've done nothing wrong and, therefore, aren't bad, or you justify your hurtful actions, expecting the explanation to excuse your behavior and win forgiveness.

When you make your actions right by excuses, you avoid admitting you were wrong. Such reasoning has a tendency to become far-fetched since you're trying to avoid a truth that everyone else can plainly see. When children get into trouble they also invent ridiculous excuses. Saying "A man came in through the window and broke the vase" may be transparently false, but it demonstrates the power of words in removing responsibility. The use of excuses by adults is different only in that the culprit is more practiced, has a better idea of what is plausible, and knows how to manipulate the other person. He may play the game much more adroitly, but his object is still the same: to avoid blame.

Because there is a basic self-deception in excuses, a person who uses them has difficulty admitting he did wrong and, therefore, can't forgive himself. Behind the explanations remains a nagging doubt about his basic goodness, and so he's prone to chronic depression. What's worse, the depression is difficult to resolve because self-forgiveness first requires an admission of wrongdoing.

There is a certain amount of blaming implied in all excuses. Some people have an excuse for everything—why they're not happy, why they haven't achieved success, why they acted in a particular way, why they lost their money, their job, their lover, or even their car keys. There are excuses for every occasion and need, but there is no excuse that will put a dishonest heart to rest.

Excuses are used to defend against a loss of personal power.

Pretending

Pretending is making believe that things are not as they are.

Pretending ranges from a student putting on airs that he is brighter than he is and would have gotten an A on his exam if he studied but instead got a C; to actually believing you are the most brilliant mind of your generation and that your flunking out of school was just to test the awareness of your professors.

Pretenses protect you from a loss of self-esteem.

Pretenses keep you from becoming embarrassed.

Pretenses stand between you and a true judging of your performance.

Pretenses also stand between you and feelings you may find uncomfortable. It's common for people to pretend they're above being hurt just to avoid dealing with anger. They split their anger away from themselves, pretending they don't own it, but it often finds expression in sudden, angry histrionics. Curiously, such people don't feel embarrassed by these angry performances, but are likely to be mortified by anything that cuts through their pretenses and reveals that they care or are vulnerable.

These three defensive patterns usually overlap. Everyone uses more than one kind of defense. No one likes to suffer, and few of us are strong enough to face reality squarely in the eye every minute of every day.

No one can blame you for acting defensively under stress. Difficulties arise when a defense doesn't yield to reality after the danger is past, but instead persists and continues to distort the way you perceive reality and interferes with your ability to adapt. Then you're likely to view the world as prejudiced against you, when the truth is that you are the one who is prejudiced.

When defenses protect you too well, your world becomes hell on earth. When denial is permitted full sway, it is impossible to tell what is real. When excuses take over, plots are projected onto the world. And when pretenses substitute for reality, the self becomes lost between wishing and hiding.

You cannot be happy if you are defensive. Happiness consists of having real needs honestly met. Defenses occlude reality and diminish your ability to savor life.

While it is not possible to become completely free of defenses, the following exercises will help you become more aware of your defensive postures so you can take them into consideration and be more flexible.

Mapping Your Emotional Blind Spots

Your blind spots are your defensive positions. We're going to determine how you defend and against what feeling. The key is to look directly at your pain and see how you avoid it. The way you avoid the truth is your defensive style.

These exercises will use three tapes: the Survey Tape you made at the very beginning, Tape II, the Feeling Tape and the Feeling Cards, and finally Tape I.

These exercises are the most difficult and frustrating work in this book. Understanding and mastering defenses are also the most difficult part of therapy. I have tried to keep the work as simple and direct as possible. Even so, it will be confusing and inaccessible at times; that is the nature of defensive action. Any effort you make here will provide you with valuable insights into the part of your behavior that is usually hidden from your awareness.

Don't expect what follows to be easy.

EXERCISE ONE

Replay the Survey Tape. As you listen to your responses, note any source of pain and the defense you used to handle it.

Indicate the pain and defenses in your notebook as follows.

Pain	Defense Used to Deal with the Feeling
Put down the feeling and its source	Is it denied, explained/excused, or treated with pretense?

When you put down the source of the pain, it's helpful to think of it as a loss of control or lovability or self-esteem. Describe the source briefly.

Question: What credit did you deserve and not receive?

Answer: I created a new filing system at work, but no one noticed. I didn't tell anyone how I felt, but later I embarrassed the boss in front of his supervisor.

This might be put down as:

Pain	Defense Used to Deal with the Feeling
Hurt over not being noticed (loss of self-esteem)	Pretended not to care. Later created a scene.

Do this for as many sources of pain as you can identify. You are doing well if you can outline ten or more in this way.

EXERCISE TWO

Take the Feeling Cards you transcribed from Tape II, the Feeling Tape, and in similar fashion take each painful feeling, and next to it indicate the defense you used to deal with it. It will help to play the tape as you work.

When you're done, examine your responses to both Exercises One and Two. Consider the following questions and compile the results in your notebook.

- What feelings are you most likely to defend against? How?
- What feeling can you experience without getting evasive?
- What feeling tends to linger? Why? What happens to it?

- How do you react to criticism, rejection, being exposed, or being at fault?
- How honest are you? When are you likely to be dishonest?
- When are you least likely to be trustworthy? Why?
- When are you most likely to hide, run, or lie?
- When do you insist on being right?

- When do you become demanding, blaming, aggressive?

- What defense(s) protect you?
- How well do they work?
- Are they rigid or flexible?
- Can you admit mistakes, weakness?
- What situations make you most defensive? Loss of love, control, self-esteem?
- What people make you defensive? Why?
- Are they family, authority, lovers, protectors, or people you take care of?
- What do you expect of them? How are you disappointed?
- Do you feel obligated to them?
- Do you think they owe you something? Why?
- Is your view reasonable?
- When are you most open, most free, most rational, most secure?
- How often does this ideal situation occur?

More than likely, you'll come across some responses that are difficult to categorize. Group these feelings and defenses together. Look at them carefully, for they're likely to be in the very center of your blind spot, especially when you're not clear-headed about reporting them.

Confusion, memory loss, or avoidance are often most intense in those areas of your life when you are most vulnerable. Study your vague reactions very carefully; they are probably a subtle form of denial. Ask yourself what pain you are avoiding by being confused. Are you afraid of being wrong or at fault? What do you have most difficulty admitting?

Any inability to deal with a feeling directly is a blind spot. Again, it is plainly visible to everyone else, most especially when you try to conceal it. Blind spots leave you wide open to anyone who knows your weakness. If you are hungry for love, you put yourself at the mercy of anyone you're attracted to. The temptation for others to use your weakness against you is always present, but it becomes overwhelming when the other person, like you, is sometimes not at his or her best and wants to control you. If you become aware of your neediness and can accept it, you will provide fewer opportunities for others to use you.

If you can accept yourself so that you can experience rejection without losing self-worth, you can experience life without self-denial.

If you can accept feeling powerless when a situation is out of control and go along with reality instead of fighting it or trying to give the impression of power, you won't have to waste your time making excuses for your impotence.

If you can accept that you are still growing and therefore have shortcomings, you won't have to pretend that you are what you are not. You can enjoy yourself as you are.

The critical step in mastering your defenses is understanding what feelings frighten you and what techniques of avoidance you habitually use. These defensive patterns were shaped in childhood, reinforced by experience, clung to out of fear and habit. They are your favorite excuses, your little games, the bad moods in which you indulge yourself. The truth is that although you've outgrown most of them, you keep these defensive toys around because you think they still work. They don't. When you finally give them up you'll wonder if they ever really did.

EXERCISE THREE

Finally, take Tape I and listen to it again. As you did in the previous two exercises, indicate the painful situations and the defenses you used in managing them.

As you answer the following questions, use the example in Exercise One as the model for evaluating these defenses and keep a similar record. It may not be possible to answer each question completely, but do the best you can.

- Can you tell when your defensive pattern began?
- What were you protecting against at that time?
- At what time were you most frightened when you were growing up? What was going on?
- What were you most ashamed of then? How did you manage the feeling?
- When did you feel the worst about yourself when you were growing up?
- When did you feel most powerless? How did you deal with this feeling?
- Did any of your defensive patterns disappear as you grew up? What happened that let you give them up?
- What defensive patterns have persisted?
- What will it take to relinquish them?

At this point you should have a grasp of the feelings that you find difficult to deal with directly and the defensive pattern you are likely to fall back on under stress.

It is useful to summarize your defensive attitudes and indicate whatever corrective action suggests itself to you. Sometimes it all boils down to a simple truth, as in the following entry.

Charlene, a forty-three-year-old interior designer, runs her business as if her actions have no consequences. She buys impulsively, ridicules her clients' tastes, changes her mind capriciously, and so creates many problems she could have avoided.

Feeling	Defense
I'm always competitive.	*I put down the*
I doubt my worth.	*competition.*
	I pretend they're no good, too.
	(See, I really do doubt my worth!)

Corrective Action
I must believe in myself. I've put in years of hard work and succeeded even if I've acted like a flake. I know I could do much better! If I want to take credit for my successes, I have to risk being blamed for my failures. I have to think things through and take responsibility for my actions.

Charlene's insight that she pretends that her success and that of her competition are just luck was a sobering realization. It changed her attitude from "what will be, will be" to "I'll get what I work for."

From now on, when you hear yourself denying, making excuses, or pretending, be aware that you're not dealing with the situation as honestly as you could. Further, ask yourself what feeling you are avoiding.

This can be the beginning of new growth. If you learn to use your understanding of your defense pattern as a guide, you will become more direct in identifying and solving problems. As a result, your life will become simpler, happier, and more open to joy.

Examining Your Attitude

A happy life is lived deliberately.

If you face negative feelings directly, they're usually fleeting. When you hide from them, these negative *feelings* can grow into negative *attitudes* that cause you to lose your direction. When you live by negative expectations, your life becomes counterfeit.

When you're unhappy, being negative *always* seems justified. The facts of your life can easily be distorted to support your outlook. When you create a negative present, you are also creating a negative past and future. You can then predict the worst with great confidence because you will make it happen.

You first learned this negative attitude when you began to speak. Learning to say "No" was a powerful discovery that you still abuse, especially when you feel reduced to being a child; that is, powerless. At such times, being negative is often the only action you feel capable of taking.

When you follow a negative point of view, you begin to see connections where none exist. Your logic is twisted as you try to justify your position. You come to believe the world is unfair when it doesn't make you happy. Your negativity separates you from the truth. It sets you up for failure.

The price you pay for a negative attitude is to feel continually undermined. You search in vain for your courage but find it has abandoned you, for courage exists only as a reaction to the truth.

It's hard to act positively if you always expect to be disappointed, but if you don't feel you deserve what you want, you won't get it.

Perhaps you feel you have good reason to be negative. It's true that there's suffering in everyone's life. Everyone has some reservations over being loved, betrayed, misunderstood, avoided, rejected by parents, but how much power this negative influence is permitted now, in this moment, is always your choice. While it may not be possible to change your past, it's always possible for you to learn to deal with the present more honestly, to believe in yourself again, to make something positive happen.

You may not have had the help or the encouragement you needed when you were growing up, but at this moment the support you need most is your own. Even if you suddenly had everything you ever lacked, your concern now would still be to keep a positive attitude. Should you one day find the life that's right for you and the perfect person to share it with, you'd still be responsible for keeping a positive outlook. Otherwise you'd soon lose it all and be back in the same old negative position.

Acting positively takes a little practice. You have to believe that good work produces good results. You must always act as if you deserve happiness and by so doing create a momentum of worthiness.

FINAL EXERCISE

In light of everything we have discussed so far, spread out your Feeling Cards and replay your Feeling Tape once again. Consider the following points and record your comments in your notebook.

- What attitudes get in your way?
- What problems would not be present if your attitude were different?
- What disappoints you? Why does it?
- Is there another way you could look at your disappointments besides taking them so personally? What stops you?
- When are you most likely to be negative?
- List all the circumstances that make you feel cheated, hurt, used, or let down. Assume that your attitude is partly responsible even if you don't believe it. Put down how you could make each situation better by changing your attitude.

The first step toward creating the life you want is to take responsibility for your attitude. You do this best by keeping current with your feelings.

Be sure to keep your Feeling Cards to use in the next part of the book.

6 | Tape III: The New Life Tape

Prepare yourself for an unusual journey. I am going to take you far away, to a place so distant you can only dream about it. Get your tape recorder and prepare to dictate. Again, you should be in a quiet room where you can have privacy.

Free your mind from any thoughts or concerns of the day. Relax.

Imagine it is morning and you are lying in bed, waking to a typical day in your life ten years from now.

That's correct. Ten years.

Before you start thinking any thoughts on your own, I want to tell you what's happened to you during these ten years.

You made it!

I think that's the most concise way of putting it. You found the courage and strength to develop and follow through on your plans. You didn't always have luck with you, but you believed in yourself, worked hard, and you stayed with it.

As I said, you made it.

You found success in your work and happiness in your personal life.

You don't believe it?

Well, if you discovered what you're naturally inclined to be and worked at it, in ten years you'd be a success beyond your fondest dreams. And that's precisely what you did!

You still don't believe it?

Are you suggesting that you'll never make it, that there's no possibility of your ever succeeding?

I want to address myself to these doubts.

I've got news for you. You have confidence in yourself now. These doubts don't exist anymore. You outgrew them long ago, so let's have no more of this disbelief.

On this particular morning we find you living the life you always wanted and being yourself, without asking permission or making excuses. You're doing what you love to do and doing it well because you're full of energy and focused on your work. You're friendly and you're busy, optimistic, and enthusiastic.

My friend, you have become a believer. You know *from experience* that if you do your best, you succeed.

If this sounds impossible, it's probably because you're still accustomed to doubting yourself. Trust that you overcame your doubts and did what you had to do to succeed.

Learning to believe in yourself was the most important thing you did in those ten years. Perhaps the most important thing you ever did. It made the difference.

Anyhow, you did it.

So put aside this old doubting and wake up this morning to a world in which you have risen to your best.

Answer all of the following questions. Even if you can't see the answer clearly, you still have some idea about the way your life could be if you gave it your best effort. Examine the reality you already know and project the best, most favorable future for yourself. Assume that it's all possible because it *is* all possible. Put down what you think, know, suspect, believe, and hope, just as it comes to you. We're trying to draw a sketch of the future to help you shape your own destiny.

Your New World

Turn on the tape recorder, read each of the following questions aloud, and dictate your answers as they come to you. Don't rush.

The morning sky is getting lighter. You can see your bedroom quite plainly.

Your Relationship

- Who is in bed next to you?
- How long have you known this person?
- How long have you lived together?
- What do you like most about this person?
- How has your relationship changed in the past ten years?

- What were the problems between you?
- What did each of you contribute to them?
- How did you settle your differences?
- How did the other person have to change?
- What made it possible for them to do so?
- What did you learn to accept about this person that couldn't be changed?
- How did you have to change?
- What made it possible for you to do so?
- What shortcomings did this person learn to accept in you?
- What feelings do you have for the person lying next to you?
- What does this person give to you?
- How does this person help you?
- How does this person respond to you?

All in all, you know you now have the relationship you want. You realize it's not perfect, but at least it allows you to be yourself.

A Recent Honor
The other person wakes up, smiles, and says, "Congratulations again on last night. I was really proud of you. You gave a wonderful acceptance speech and you deserved the honor."

- What is your partner referring to?
- Explain your achievement in detail.
- What was this award and what did it mean to you?
- Were you surprised to receive it or was it your goal?
- Who were your closest competitors?
- Why were you picked?

Around the House

You can't lie around all morning. Today is an especially busy day. You get up and open the curtains.

- Describe the view from your bedroom window.
- Where is this? In town? In the country?
- Exactly what place?
- How long have you lived here?
- Do you have another home anywhere? If so, where?
- What do you do there?
- Walk through your home and describe the rooms you live in and how you furnished them. Take your time and provide details.

Friends and Family

You enter your study. On the wall above your desk is a collection of photographs taken during the last ten years. Some were taken when you were on vacation.

- Who is in those vacation pictures?
- Where did you go last year?
- The year before that?

There are also pictures of everyone in your family here.

- Tell who is in each picture, what they are all doing now, and how well they turned out.
- Tell what each had to overcome and the part you played in their success.
- Tell when and where each picture was taken.

There are also pictures of old friends.

- Who are they?

- What are they doing now?
- How often do you see these people?
- What do they mean to you?

There are also some new friends, people you've only met recently but who have become very close to you.

- Who are these people?
- What is the basis of your friendship?
- What do you get from them?
- What do you give them?
- What is the difference between your new and old friends?

A Productive Life

As I said, you've achieved success on your own terms. You've found the work that you like and you no longer have financial problems.

You look at your schedule. Your first appointment is a meeting to discuss the final plans for an important project that you've been working on for some time.

- What is the project you're going to discuss today?
- Describe your work situation. What do you do? How, where, and when?
- With whom are you meeting this morning?
- What will you be talking about?
- Who else do you work with?
- What do they do for you?
- How long did it take you to accomplish the work you were just honored for? Give a brief history of the best results of your work these past ten years. Start by saying that you achieved success, how you did it, and what it feels like being here.

- Did you have any idea where you were headed when you started out?
- How and when did you first discover what you were supposed to be doing?
- When did you finally start taking yourself seriously?
- What led up to it?
- What was the critical turning point?
- What other projects have you worked on? Describe in detail the work involved in each.
- What do you hope each will become?
- What obstacles lie ahead? How do you plan to deal with them?

Lunch

Your meeting is productive, but you cut it short because today you're having an important lunch.

- Is it a business or social lunch?
- Who will be there?
- Who arranged it?
- What does the other person expect?
- What do you want to happen?
- What does happen?

The Afternoon

The rest of the afternoon is more like your usual day.

- How do you spend it?
- With whom did you meet?
- What did they do for you?
- What did they want from you?
- In what other activities besides work are you involved?
- Where did you stop on the way home and what did you do there?

- What form of transportation did you take?
- Describe your neighborhood.
- What does your home look like?
- Who else lives with you?
- What have they been doing all day?
- Are they happy?
- How did they find their contentment?

The Risks You Took

You feel reflective and spend a few private moments in your study considering how far you've come.

- What were the important risks you took during the past ten years?
- When did you put yourself on the line and reach for something better?

All of the success you've achieved came as the result of taking a risk. Dictate all the risks you took to get where you are, personal, career, and family.

For each risk you took in the past ten years, explain:

- What goal you sought.
- What the most difficult part of the risk was.
- What you did to make sure it went your way.
- How you found the courage to take it.

In every risk, you have to leave something behind, just as when you cross a river you leave one bank to get to the other. It's the fear of losing that slows you down. You fear losing love, control, and respect. For each of your risks, indicate:

- What you gave up to move ahead.
- Who was hurt when you risked.
- How that happened.

- If it could have been prevented.
- How it finally turned out for these people.

Some people couldn't accept your growing. Obviously they had their own problems.

- Who disapproved of you or withheld their support?
- Who belittled your attempts?
- Who blocked you?
- What were the greatest obstacles in your path?
- How did you get over them? Remember that you did overcome them.
- Did you stand up to others?
- Did you leave the company, the marriage the friendship, the profession?
- How did you finally do it?

A Private Celebration

This evening you're throwing a party to thank people for their support. You've invited everyone who's helped you during the past twenty years.

Dictate your guest list and indicate what each person has done for you.

Remember that no one did your work for you. You never would have become successful if you hadn't found your strength and done it on your own. Other people may have opened doors, but you had to knock on them and make believers and supporters out of strangers. When you think of whom you'd like to befriend and invite to your party, don't be inhibited by their importance. Put their name down. If they had a necessary role to play, assume you got to meet them. As you dictate each name, also indicate how you made contact with them. You'd be surprised at how right your first instincts are.

At the party, someone who has known you for many years makes a little speech praising your efforts, telling how you built your success and listing your achievements. He ends by mentioning a few of your close calls. You are amused.

Dictate this speech.

As you consider how far you've come, you realize how much more honest you are now than you used to be. One of the biggest changes you made was to stop selling out.

Selling Out

Selling out is taking a path you wouldn't take if you were free to follow your best interests. It is a lesser way of being because when you give up part of yourself you become less. Such self-defeating choices are made out of the fear that you're not good enough to get what you want, so you take whatever's offered to you. When you don't do what's best for you, you make that fear a reality. Rather than please yourself, you try to please someone else in the hope that winning approval will make you feel better.

Sometimes, out of desperation, you lower your goals or seek to acquire material possessions, power, or money, trying to impress others when you can't satisfy yourself.

The material gains you sold out for lack one necessary quality. They don't fulfill you. So you're forced to hide from your unhappiness by acquiring still more or to seek continual reassurance that you were wise to do what you did. You never feel right about yourself when you sell out.

Compromising is not the same as selling out. A compromise is a yielding exchange between two points of view with the intention of finding the most workable direction; selling out is giving in to your doubting, weaker self, to your pessimism, to the soul that has forgotten how to dream.

If you believe you're better off after selling out, it's because you must believe that. You exclude the truth from your world and so it grows smaller to contain your narrow vision. You're looking for support. Even blind, lip-serving support works for you when you've sold out, to say nothing about your being susceptible to flattery and insincere or fulsome praise. None of this satisfies you because in your heart you know the truth. You're not doing what makes you happy.

When you sell out, you pursue the wrong lovers, take the wrong jobs, move to the wrong city, marry the wrong person, and have children for the wrong reason. All because you refuse to accept yourself as you are and take responsibility for making yourself complete.

When you sell out, you become cynical. You believe that because you betrayed yourself and became hard, everyone else did too. You also suspect that everyone is a phony. You put distance between yourself and the positive parts of life. You focus on what supports your alibi for not living the life you wanted.

If you think money will solve all your problems, you're wrong. Money buys distraction, not personal worth. Although the contrast from poor to rich is heady and arrests your attention by creating a false sense of confidence, any feelings of inadequacy persist and eventually return to have their say.

The worst part about selling out is that it reinforces your belief that you aren't as good as you are. When you sell out for security, you think you're taking out insurance against fate, but you're really betting you won't make it on your own. Giving away a piece of your future is hardly protecting yourself. Your belief in yourself is the difference between success and just holding on. When you abandon responsibility, you weaken your will.

Will comes from knowing that you are doing what is right.

Self-confidence grows out of acting in your best interests when you have to.

Living life to the fullest, working hard, and taking your chances is the only way to be safe.

In the end, no one wins who hasn't risked everything.

When you sell out, you give up your chances for making your greatest contribution. You always know this somewhere deep inside, and even if you can't look at it, it will find dark moments to speak to you and bring you to the depths of sadness. Then the truth will stand unopposed, whisper your unworthiness to your heart, and break it with remembered regrets.

Peace of mind is knowing that you did what you had to do.

Let's consider the errors of your past, how you used to sell yourself short, before you decided to change.

The following questions are a bit tricky because they ask you to be honest about your dishonesties. In answering them you are referring to your past, not your future. Dictate your immediate answers. Just say what comes into your mind.

- What did you sell out for?
- When did you give too much away?
- What did you hope to gain?
- What was your price? Was it a job, a love, a title?
- What was your weakness? What couldn't you resist—drugs, alcohol, sex, money, gambling, fame, food, power, or being neurotic?

Maybe you could have resisted selling out if you had tried, but you didn't.

- Were you bound?
- What obligated you? A promise? An expectation?
- Were you upholding the family name?
- Was it honor?

If you're like the rest of us, you sold out more than once, out of fear, love, loneliness, but mostly out of a lack of belief in yourself.

- When did you act against your better judgment?
- When did you abandon your dream?
- Why didn't you do what you wanted?
- How did it hurt you?
- How did it all work out?
- Would you do it again?
- Which of your big decisions would you change if you could? Just dictate these as fast as you can.
- Is there any way you can correct your mistakes?

Obstacles Overcome
I'm interested in your success, especially your gains against adversity. There are moments of triumph in every life. I want to know yours. Answer these ques-

tions both from the vantage point of ten years in the future and also from your perspective on the past.

Most people accomplish a great deal, unnoticed and without fanfare. You've gotten someplace even if your arrival was not celebrated.

Dictate the accomplishments you're most proud of. Start with the earliest ones you remember, the times when you struggled to attain something and succeeded.

For each accomplishment, indicate:

- What it meant to you and what it proved about you.
- What you had to overcome—doubts, self-pity, laziness, fear of failure, other attitudes, other people. Tell what you overcame and how you did it.
- How long did it take?
- Who helped you?
- How important was that help?
- What did you learn about yourself in your struggle?
- Where did you find the courage to change?

When people wish they were more than they are, they exaggerate their worth and try to sell themselves to others. They avoid looking at themselves because they're afraid of seeing their shortcomings. And because they've held themselves out to be more than they are, when they do achieve something, they're often disappointed that the gain wasn't greater. It's easy to lose perspective when you don't accept yourself as you are.

The way your life is is exactly the way it should be. Because you reacted the way you did to what happened to you, you became what you are. There is an undeniable logic to reality. Reality is the way things are, not what they should have been or might be. So you must know what you want and be free to act. Otherwise you won't be happy.

All this is simply suggesting to you the value of a goal. Everyone needs a direction to believe in, something worth risking for. If you know you are on the road to a destination that will make you happy, you can act in confidence. When you are on your way, you can delight in any accomplishment, no matter how small, because you realize every advance brings you closer to victory. Having a goal helps you make decisions.

Because you know what's important, you know when it's safe to yield and when you must stand your ground.

If you have goals, your life is filled with little successes.

Any time you accept a new part of yourself, you gain.

Any time you understand something new, you are a victor.

Any time you feel compassion for another person's pain, you grow along with them.

There's a good reason why you have difficulty facing obstacles. Whenever you confront an impasse or reach beyond your usual grasp, you're reminded of yourself when you were young.

Even if you had the most giving and loving parents, your life as a child was filled with the unknown and untried. Dependent on the love and support of others, you became torn between doing what you wanted and the fear of rejection. Potential dangers were everywhere. Testing out the world meant measuring yourself as well. Sometimes curiosity and exploration resulted in injury or reprimand. Life felt pretty rough. You had no prior experience to give you courage and few diversions to dilute the pain. When you failed, you felt like a total failure. No wonder you often felt helpless. The obstacles you faced as a child may not seem great now, but they influenced your present attitude toward risking. As a result, every new challenge has the potential to awaken those old feelings of helplessness and the fear of failure.

All growth involves pain and, therefore, anxiety. Don't be afraid of fear when you have a new challenge. It only means that what you're risking is meaningful to you. Allow your fear to motivate you. Your fear tells you to treat the situation as if it matters. That is why taking a risk arrests your attention. You fear for your worth.

Your Defeats

When you look back on all that's happened to you, you can see the struggles that didn't turn out the way you wanted. The times you failed are as important to understand as the times you won. This group of questions is not intended to dishearten you but to give you new insight into the path you followed.

Starting with childhood and going right up to the present, what defeats did you suffer? Dictate them.

- What did you lose in each one?
- Did any loss get the best of you? How?
- How did you recover?
- Did you try again? Why not?

- Was the loss replaceable? How did you cope with it if it wasn't?
- What part did you play in bringing on the loss?
- Who else was to blame?
- What lessons did you learn?
- Do you still wonder how your life might have been if not for a particular defeat?
- Is it still possible to try again?
- What holds you back?

Breaking Away

But you've come quite a distance from those early times. In these ten years you've made a success of most of your setbacks. Just look at your work, how you live, this party for instance. From this future vantage point, answer the following questions about this projected future decade:

- What mistakes did you correct in order to get on the right track?
- How did you come to realize and repair each mistake?
- List the difficult people you had to manage. (Note: Most of the people in your future are involved with you now.)
- Who did you finally break with and when?

If you believe that there's no point at which you would break from someone, it suggests that you don't value yourself enough to separate from a destructive force, so let's put it another way.

- What people in your life would you like to break away from today but can't?

- Why can't you?
- Name each person and dictate your reason for holding on. It's important.

Since you did make it, we know that you finally succeeded in getting away from these people.

- How did you do it in each case?
- What gave you the courage to let go? Was it the love and support of another person? The belief in a better goal, a better life?
- What finally permitted you to do what was best for you? Be specific.

Supports

Although you'd like to believe you don't need anyone, especially when you feel discouraged or bitter, no one ever makes it totally alone. Everyone begins life as an ignorant primitive and builds on the work of others.

You admire good, brave, daring, and accomplished people because you see some of the same qualities in yourself and identify with their success and struggle. Heroes are receptacles for your yearning. They are proof that personal dreams can come true, that struggles can be won and disadvantages conquered. Heroes speak to the good within you and bid you to be your best.

Look over the guest list for your party, think about your life, and dictate your answers to the following questions:

- Whom did you model yourself after?
- How did they inspire you?
- Who encouraged you? How?
- What difference did it make?

- What gave each of these people the special power to influence you?
- Name all the people you admire most, living, dead or historical, and tell what you admire in each of them.

The Gifts You Gave

Sometimes it's hard to remember the important role you played in the lives of others. Consider for a moment all those you have helped in the past as well as all the people your success in the future has permitted you to help. Dictate the names on that list.

For each person indicate:

- What you gave.
- The difference it made.
- The pleasure you got from giving.
- How aware the other person was of your part.
- How they showed their appreciation.
- Did you have any feeling of being used or taken for granted?
- How would you categorize your gift: material presents, support and understanding, money, or constructive criticism?
- What was your style of giving in each case: free, conditional, obligated, guilty, manipulative, controlling?
- What did you expect to gain from each person?

Acknowledging the Inevitable

The essence of growing is recognizing the futility of a hopeless enterprise or false belief and letting go of it. You hold on to what you think works for you. When a job, relationship, or attitude no longer suits you, you often still cling to it out of fear of the unknown and the unsettling suspicion that you might not be capable of doing any better. Acknowledging defeat is central to achieving success. No one is right all the time. And last year's brilliant decision can be this year's burden. So corrections must be made. You need to give up what no longer makes sense for you. Getting better depends on it.

Look back on these ten years in the future and reflect on what you gave up to get where you are. Dictate your responses.

- What dream, person, or beliefs did you give up?
- What else did you let go of in these ten years?
- Tell how each one inhibited you.
- How badly were you hurt before you acted?
- Why did you wait as long as you did?
- Whose feelings did you put ahead of your own?
- What did you hope to accomplish by doing so? Did it work out?
- What else did you let get in your way?
- How did you remove these interferences?

Improvements

Still, much of your success in these ten years in the future has depended on making up for what you lacked as well as letting go of what no longer worked. Take your time to answer the following questions carefully. Be specific and explain in detail.

- What deficiencies did you correct?
- What strengths did you acquire?
- How did you do it?

- What education did you get? Where? How long did it take?
- What skills did you learn?
- How else did you improve youself?
- What made it possible for you to take these steps?
- What was the turning point that made you decide?

Parting Shots

Your party is drawing to an end. Friends, family and associates have all drifted out into the night, leaving you and the person you live with sitting together on the living room couch. A flashbulb startles you. It's a magazine photographer, taking a last shot. As he puts his equipment away, the reporter with him asks if you would mind answering a few final questions. Even though you've been asked them before you consent, but you insist on answering briefly and quickly. Dictate these responses as well.

- How much money are you worth?
- What was the biggest break in your life?
- Are you happy?
- What are you doing next?
- How are your kids?
- What is the biggest mistake you ever made?
- What is your weakness?
- Are you faithful?
- What belief gives you your strength?
- Of what accomplishment are you most proud?
- What are you ashamed of?
- Is there any moment you'd like to live over again?
- Is there any moment you'd like to forget?
- To whom do you owe the most?
- What was the single most important factor in your success?

In the morning you are going away on a well-deserved vacation.

- Where are you going? With whom and for how long?

Enough of these questions. You've got a busy day tomorrow.

Tape III: Analytical Workbook—The Action Board, Creating Your Future

In this workbook we're going to create an Action Board that defines your goals and develops a plan for reaching them. We'll examine your wants, strengths, and needs and find the plan that has the best chances for success. I'll try to make the work as easy as possible. Be as open as you can in completing the work of each section.

The Action Board is a simple device for creating a visual display of problems, goals, feelings, and conflicts. I use it to organize my own work. I teach my patients to use it to gain perspective and order. It's a valuable concept that will make your life smoother and more directed. Much of what the Action Board does is subliminal in nature. Once it is complete, it is effective by its presence alone. It organizes your activities and puts them into context. It provides a frame of reference for measuring your efforts, showing where corrections and adjustments need to be made. It also serves as a reminder, telling what needs to be done at each step in a project as well as indicating when new steps need to be developed. When it is completed, you'll have a bulletin board with each of your goals stated on a card and the immediate Next Steps necessary to reach them indicated on a card below.

You'll need several hundred 3-by-5 cards, a wide-tipped felt marker, some pushpins, and a bulletin board. I suggest you use any flat surface. A 3-by-5 card file with index cards will also come in handy.

As we develop your Action Board in the following sections, the way it works will become clearer.

Be patient; you're going to be writing out hundreds of 3-by-5 cards. It'll seem like a lot of work at first, but with time it will get easier. Be sure to save all the cards you make; they will be used many times.

If a particular question or topic doesn't seem to apply to you, there is still much to gain by considering its implications. The examples of Action Boards that I offer may not appear to follow these directions perfectly. They don't. They are adapted to suit the needs of the person in each example. In the hundreds of patients I've studied, I have never seen two identical Action Boards. You must adapt this system to fit your needs. This guide is designed to be flexible. The devices and categories that follow will attempt to define your direction, but you may find some issues only of passing interest while other subjects will hold your attention for days. You need follow only the general plan offered here. Make whatever changes you need to make it work for you.

Defining the Gap Between Present and Future

Always read through the instructions section *before* you replay Tape III, the New Life Tape. As you listen, you should have a notebook and stack of 3-by-5 cards nearby.

Use the notebook to put down any observations, trends, or ideas that come to mind that are not specifically asked for in these workbooks. At this point, the most important discoveries will be made by you without any prompting from me. After all, you now know yourself very well.

In this replay, you'll be concerned with the difference between your life in the present and your life in the future. Play the tape. Reflect on this future life. Think how you would feel if the life being described were yours today.

Improvement Cards

As you listen to the tape, put down every improvement in your life that you hear, such as "more meaningful work." Use a different 3-by-5 card for each one. Label each card "Improvement" in the upper-right-hand corner.

When you finish completing these cards, turn them over and on the back indicate what each Improvement depends upon, such as, "Being in business for myself; doing what I want." Label the back "Improvement Key."

Then turn the cards over again and arrange the Improvements in order of importance to you, putting first the one you think would make you the happiest. Summarize these Improvements on a single card if you can.

Source Cards

Get the Feeling Cards you made when you transcribed Tape II, the Feeling Tape, and remove the cards describing your positive feelings. These cards reflect the sources of pleasure in your present life. Examine the events that made you happy and copy each one onto a 3-by-5 card. Label these cards "Sources."

Look at these Sources. Consider the satisfaction you felt in each situation. Was it personal fulfillment, achieving, being given to, giving, being loved, loving someone, or seeing another person being fulfilled? Consider the kind of gratification you felt. Indicate the Needs that were fulfilled by each Source on the back of each Source card. Label the back "Needs."

Arrange your Source cards in order of the pleasure you derived from them. Now write "My Happiness Depends On" on a 3-by-5 card and pin it up on the top left of your Action Board. Then pin up the Source cards in order directly below.

Now pin up the Improvement cards again in order of their importance on the right side of the Action Board. Compare the two columns. Your present sources of pleasure should have some relevance to the improvements you hope to make in the future.

If there is no correlation, it means that you were being unrealistic when you described the future. True happiness is based on reality. The things that make you happy today are not that different from what made you happy years ago and won't be that different from what will make you happy years from now. Your needs don't change that much, but the way you fulfill them can change considerably.

Turn over the Source cards now, making a row of your Needs on the Action Board.

- Which needs repeat?
- Are the needs you thought most important at the top of the row?

■ Is the pleasure in the future consistent with your present needs being met?

Defining Steps

Turn the Needs over once again so the Sources face you.

Look at the gap between your pleasure today and what you want to have ten years from now. See if you can define any Steps that would take you from the cards on the left to those on the right.

■ What would you need to do to get where you want?

Put down on 3-by-5 cards anything that comes into your mind that might help you close this gap. Label these cards "Steps" and post them in the middle.

■ Which of your Sources must you preserve to be happy in the future?

Too often people don't realize how well off they are and so take unnecessary risks. Become aware of what makes you happy now so you won't take needless chances.

Don't worry if there seem to be too many or too few cards. We're just beginning to shape a direction. Don't be alarmed if the direction seems impossibly confused or highflown. It is just an idea. At this point we are including every possibility.

This is the early Action Board of Candice, a promising twenty-six-year-old actress who had always been dependent on her father's approval and had been afraid to risk because success signified being on her own. Even at this early stage, the Action Board helped Candice discover that she was more organized and goal-directed than she had realized.

Sources of Pleasure

Summary:

Doing a good job fulfills me

Good audition at Universal

Praise from director

Fan in lobby praising my non-Equity performance

Needs

To do my work well

To be loved by public, admired by colleagues!

Summary

Personal contacts are very important to me!

I need approval.

Steps I Need

New agent

More singing lessons

Acting lessons; who's best?

Need a business manager

Find original properties and get a writer to adapt them for me

New approach—maybe form my own production company

Improvements

Summary:

1. Better, Bigger Roles
2. To Approve of Myself More

Academy Award (I can dream, can't I?)

Offered best roles without reading for them

Opening on Broadway

Being the toast of Europe

Improvement Keys

Pay attention to every detail.

Need a manager who believes in me!

Believe in myself.

Work like a dog.

Obstacles

We are going to define the obstacles that stand in your way. Remove all the cards from your Action Board, keeping them in order.

Play the New Life Tape.

As you listen, note every person who made your life more difficult. Put each name on a separate index card and directly below indicate how each interfered. Label these "Obstacles."

Put down any other Obstacles you notice. Again, put each one on a separate 3-by-5 card; indicate how each blocks you, from what, and how you might get rid of it. These obstacles need not be people.

Pin these Obstacles on the Action Board. Examine them in light of the following questions.

- If an obstacle were removed from your life, what difference would that make?
- Would it make you afraid? How?

If the removal of an obstacle would bring on a painful feeling, one motivation for keeping the obstacle would be to prevent that feeling.

- What power does each obstacle have over you?
- What could you do for yourself to diminish the influence of each obstacle?
- Why do you permit these obstacles to stand in your way?
- Who manipulates you?
- How do they do that?
- Why don't you say "No"?
- What prevents you from protecting yourself?
- How do you allow yourself to be used?

■ What do you think of the person who permits these obstructions to affect your life?

Correcting Your Deficiencies

As you listen to the tape, you will realize that in order to get as far as you did in those ten years, you had to overcome many deficiencies.

Put down each deficiency you overcame on an index card and indicate what you did to make up for it. Tell how you started, how long it took, and what you accomplished. I want you to realize now what you must do to fix up your life, to get where you want, to have a career that fits you, and to be happy. What did you do to make this happen? Indicate the different ways you grew.

Label these cards "Deficiencies." Summarize them on a single card and set them aside.

Your Attitude

Your attitude is the single most important factor in overcoming these obstacles and deficiencies. In the end, your attitude determines your success. When the chips are down, the right attitude generates the best effort.

■ How would you characterize the attitude of the person on the tape? Realistic, pessimistic, optimistic, desperate, needy, or doubting?
■ What is this person's justification for holding this attitude?

Put down your description of this person's attitude on a 3-by-5 card and label it "Point of View." Post it on the Action Board.

- Is the attitude you described the way you see yourself?
- How does it differ? Why?

Remember to use your notebook! Your realizations about this work are always important.

Melissa is a forty-six-year-old office worker who never lived up to her early academic promise. She spends most of her time feeling sorry for herself. Unfortunately, she never does anything to make her situation any better. She wastes time, blames her co-workers when she fails, or dissolves into overstated self-blaming tantrums. The following entry was made shortly after she received an extremely poor work evaluation. It shocked her!

Sunday, very late: I'm dreading going back to work tomorrow. I feel so stuck. I struggled all weekend with this Action Board, trying to get moving. I guess I'm realizing that all these years I've been blaming my parents for standing in my way, for not sending me to college. The truth is, they didn't know any better. I knew better all the time, but chose to attack them instead of getting the education I needed. I've been so angry at them I didn't feel I deserved to succeed. Maybe I failed as an adult to make my parents feel bad about the job they did. Except they have no idea about any of this, and I'm the one who suffers! I also expect my supervisor to come to me and ask if I need help. I know this is unrealistic. Looking at all these cards, I realize that I'm my biggest obstacle. I never take chances. I guess my reluc-

tance to work at the Action Board has been to avoid admitting that. My Point of View card reads: "I shall not be moved." I've got to do something about this before it's too late. I need to become my own parent and educate myself.

Sample Action Board at this Stage

Allen is a forty-five-year-old businessman who has been in a dozen different businesses in the past eight years. He never plans for the future, has a secret dread that he's incompetent, and tries to avoid any situation where he might fail. Consequently, he is a poor decision-maker and is continually on the brink of insolvency.

Obstacles	To Correct Deficiencies	Attitude
Not enough money	Acquire only top selling lines	Desperate when I'm flat
Lousy credit line	Clean up debts (probably use a consolidating loan)	Cocky when I'm flush
Help that steals		Blame others
Low customer acceptance of products		Easily discouraged
Slow deliveries	Streamline my operation	
Always in a start-up situation	Stay with one project until it's done!	
So I never get established!		

Summary

I need to become a self-starter.

I *react* too impulsively and change plans.

I need professional financial counseling (never admitte
that before).

Who am I kidding? My problem is my attitude! I give up
too easily.

> *Even at the beginning, the Action Board can provia
> a sobering confrontation. Don't be discouraged i,
> you discover something negative about yourself. I,
> you learn what you must fix, it's a positive step.*

Locating Your Strengths and Weaknesses

This exercise was designed to be completed without
using any tapes. However, if you wish, you may use
Tape III as a reference. Each of the following sections
is a general question or a question with many possible
answers. Take the time to give as complete a response
as you can.

Write down each answer on a separate 3-by-5 card
as quickly as you think of it. Number the cards in the
order they come to mind.

WHAT WERE YOU DESIGNED TO DO?
What was nature's intent on fashioning you the way
she did? (Don't get into a lengthy philosophical discussion, weighing the meaning of existence and your role
in the universal order of things.) What are you supposed to do here? What is your life's purpose?

Are you doing what you really want or are you just
hoping that the direction you've chosen for yourself
will work out? Is there within you some hidden wish or
yearning to be doing something else? Ignore the fact

...ssible. Just write each notion down
...rd.

...you ever dreamed of becoming? This
... seem repetitive, but if you could live
...ver and be anything you wanted, what
... become?

...each of your answers "Notions."

CHANCES

...oking over your life, there were opportunities that
...ou missed. What chances should you have taken but
didn't? Limit these answers to ten or so. Put each on
its own card.

Immediately below, indicate the difference it would
have made if you had taken the chance.

On the back of each card, indicate why you didn't
take the chance.

Label the front of these cards "Chances" and the
back, "Excuses."

SUCCESS

Write down all the important successes you achieved.
Again, one success to a card. On the back of each
card, write down its key: luck, timing, hard work, talent. Be specific. If you can't think of any successes,
you're not being fair to yourself. Try again.

Label the front of these cards "Successes," the
back, "Key to Success."

FAILURES

Do the same for your failures, the times when you
tried but didn't achieve your goals. I know this is uncomfortable, but indicate the ten or so most important

failures. On the back, in a word or two, tell what went wrong. Be honest. Admit your part.

Label these cards "Failures," and the back, "Key to Failures."

PRAISE

Put down the most important compliments and praise you ever received. Write down the exact words, who said them, the circumstances, and the impact they had on you.

Label these cards "Praise."

CRITICISM

Write down the most telling criticisms you received, the ones that really cut through you, that still stick in your mind. Again, try to recall the exact words, speaker, and circumstance. Note how you felt at the time, whether you thought the criticism was true, and if you took it to heart. Take your time with this. If you can't think of serious criticisms, put down minor criticisms.

Label these cards "Criticisms."

PEOPLE YOU ADMIRE

Put down the names of the ten living people you admire most. Again, number them in the order they come to mind. On the back of each card, indicate what you consider to be the key to their success.

Also put down the names of ten people in history you'd like to have been. Indicate why in one or two words, such as love, power, talent, fame. And on the back of the card put the key to their success.

Label all of these cards "Models," and the backs, "Keys to Model's Success."

GIFTS

Put each of the most important gifts you gave on a card. Indicate why and to whom you gave them and the difference each made.

Label these "Gifts," and arrange them in order of importance to you.

FREE CHOICES

If you were totally free and had the means to do everything you wanted, what would you do? Make out a card for each of them and label them "Free Choices."

Discovering Your Best Self

Within every person there is a best self, capable of goodness, with the power to be free and loving. This inner self reflects your finest and brightest energy. Whatever stands in its way, whatever keeps this energy from expressing itself, is not good for you.

The following exercises will help you get a clearer picture of your higher self as well as the forces that obstruct you.

For each of these exercises, start with a clear Action Board. After you put the cards in place, get comfortable and sit where you can see the entire board at once. Move the cards around. Feel free to change their order or write additional cards. Your goal is to discover your truest identity, a self you can trust because it's really you. If you see something missing, add it. If a card is exaggerated or otherwise distorted, correct it or write a new one. The Action Board is your device. It is only a general guide. It's up to you to refine it and make it reflect your true intentions and real identity.

Exercise One: Defining Your Achilles Heel

Let's look at the forces that intrude on your freedom and limit your growth. It's important that you don't merely lament your imperfections, but learn to deal with them by expecting to improve. You deserve to have a positive attitude even about situations that didn't work out.

Take the Failure cards and pin them up in a column in the middle of the board with the most painful failure on top. Look at these cards for a few minutes.

- Can you see any similarities in these failures?
- Did you quit too soon? Did you hang on too long?
- Were you unprepared? Were you overconfident?
- Did you panic, act impulsively or too rigidly?
- Were you blind to problems, deaf to advice?

Summarize these failures on a single Failure Summary card and pin it at the top of the failure column.

Pin up the Criticism cards in a column to the left of the Action Board so that the most telling remarks are at the top.

- Is there a common theme to the criticism?
- Does a particular criticism repeat?
- Taking your clue from these criticisms, what does this person need to correct? What flaws do these comments point to?

Summarize these criticisms on a single Criticism Summary card and pin it at the top of the criticism column.

Now put the Chances cards on the right side of the board. Study them carefully. Consider the following:

- Do any chances repeat?
- What is this person afraid of losing?
- What does he allow to stand in his way?
- How did each failure to risk hurt him?
- How can this situation be repaired?

Summarize the Chances on a single card.

Look at the way the cards on the board relate to each other.

If you'd taken the criticisms to heart, would the failures have occurred?

What do the criticisms tell you about the person who failed? Compare the Criticism cards with the Chance cards. What do other people see as your shortcomings? Do those shortcomings have anything to do with the fear that inhibits you from risking? In other words, are you ever afraid of proving your critics correct?

Turn over the Chance cards and study the Excuses you gave for not risking. Compare these Excuses to the Criticisms. Consider:

- How does your view of yourself differ from that of your critics?
- What do you blame?
- What do they blame?
- How do you account for the difference?

Summarize and characterize your Excuses on a single card and post it at the top of the Excuse column.

Now, turn over the Failure cards and examine the issues you identified as the Key Factors in your failures. Summarize these as well. How do they compare to the criticism you've received?

How do your excuses for not risking relate to the

keys for your failure? The way the rows of cards differ and agree can provide you with another view of your blind spot. They reveal your weakness and how you react before and after a threat.

Now assume that you have just walked into the room and see this bulletin board with all these telling cards. Ask yourself:

- What sort of person does this represent?
- Where and when is this person likely to get into trouble?
- How does he make things worse?
- If you wanted to cause trouble for this person, how would you go about it?
- What simple actions could this person take to make his life better?
- Does this person take responsibility for his share of failures or does he blame others? Where is he most likely to avoid blame? What is he afraid of, then?
- What lessons does this person have to learn?
- What keeps him from learning them?

Summarize the problems that this person struggles against. Give at least three statements of advice, put each on a separate card, label them "Lessons to Learn," and post them. Study this board. Leave it up for a few days. Add to it. Let it have an impact on you. Keep notes on your reactions to it in your notebook.

You are looking at the sorts of difficulties you're most likely to encounter and the type of problems you have dealing with them.

This is the Action Board of Andrew, a fifty-five-year-old highly successful businessman, who is so goal-

Criticisms	Failures/Keys to Failures	Success/Keys to Success	Chances
Summary			
I use people	Lost race for Congress/ Wanted to prove to Dad I was important	Made money in real estate/Greed	I took every chance
I push too hard	My divorce/Wanted to prove to Louise I was great, but she just didn't care. She just wanted affection. I'm not affectionate!	Investments/Greed	I always risked
	The Stanholpe Case/I was overconfident!	I'm head of my own law firm/Proving I was smart	

directed that he overwhelms anyone or anything standing in his way. His recent divorce has stunned him. Notice that he doesn't follow the directions, but needs to include his successes in order to balance his failures.

Andrew's Notebook:

> *I'm always trying to prove something to someone.*

> *I never do anything just to please myself. I want to be on top! It's lonely at the top, though I can accept that. There's only room for one!*

> *Still, I want respect. I want other people to like me. I just don't know how to win them over. You'd think they'd be impressed and want to be my friend. They're not!*

> *I guess I don't trust myself. Sad statement to make for someone who's worth eight figures!*

> *If this is success, why doesn't it feel like success?*

Andrew's Action Board has given him the first realization that he's missing something. This is a positive step even if he feels bad about it. This is precisely what is meant by the therapist's adage that sometimes one has to feel worse before getting better. Andrew uses people and finds the world a cold place because he never fulfills himself. He never asks himself what would make him happy. He only asks what will make money for him.

Action Board exercises can be very revealing in other, unexpected ways. Take for example this notebook entry of Felix, a thirty-two-year-old sur-

veyor, who became bogged down in all the cards he created.

> *I am embarrassed to admit this, but I was unable to get all my Excuses on the board at the same time. I had more than thirty-five. I have excuses for everything, but I have no excuse for having so many Excuses! I realized that I try so hard to give the impression of being perfect that I can never admit my mistakes.*
>
> *Dad used to tell me that I never learned my lessons. I just now understood what he meant!*
>
> *How could I learn my lessons if I didn't admit my mistakes?*
>
> *I blame everyone but myself. Why couldn't I see this before? My surveyor's instruments are always in need of repair (I treat them so roughly they are always getting out of alignment). Maybe I do this to have an excuse for my errors!*
>
> *I really have been doing terrible things to myself!*

Have faith and keep working on these exercises. Do the best job you can and assemble the most coherent Action Board you can make. Study your board carefully. Often the problem in creating your board will directly illuminate other problems in your life. It is an excellent opportunity to learn, so be patient. Examine the board with the attitude that it was created by a stranger you are trying to understand. You'll be surprised at what you'll discover. If you get stuck, take a few days off. A little distance helps.

When you have completed Exercise One, remove the cards from the board, keeping them in order.

Exercise Two: Locating Your Strengths
Take the Success cards and pin them up in the center of the board in order of their importance. Look at these successes for a moment. Consider how you feel looking at them. Write down your responses in your notebook.

- Did you deserve these successes? Are you proud?
- What motivated you to succeed?
- What could you have done to make your successes even stronger?
- Is some success missing? What is it?

Pin the Praise cards up in a column to the left of the Success cards.

- Which of your abilities were responsible for your successes?
- What abilities need cultivating or further study?
- What abilities do you receive praise for, but don't use in your successes? Why? How can you use them?
- Which of your abilities go unnoticed?
- Why don't you risk revealing them?

Pin up the Gifts you gave to the right of your Successes. Look at this collection of positive elements. They represent your strength.

- What does this board say about the person who made it?
- What is this person capable of becoming?
- What could this person be hired to do?

Turn over the Success cards and look at the Keys to this person's achievements.

Identify the most important factors in his/her success.

Summarize them on a single card and post it on the board. Label this "Success Summary."

Compare the Gifts to the Successes and Praise.

- What does this person give? To whom? Why? When?
- What does he/she expect in return?
- How freely were these gifts given?
- Are people obligated to him/her in any way?
- How important is being thanked and appreciated?
- What part does being recognized play in the act of giving?

Summarize the Praise, the Gifts, and the Successes. Put each summary on a single card and post them on the Action Board. Whatever you achieve in life will probably be related to the cards you see before you. These are your established strengths. Keep them in mind. They represent you at your best.

Exercise Three: A Sense of Personal Destiny

Start with a clear board. Pin up the Free Choices in a column. Can you determine:

- What holds this person back from doing what he/she wants and why?
- What does this person secretly want to do?
- How close is your present life to realizing these free choices?
- How can these wishes become a reality?

Summarize your Free Choices on a single card.

Pin up the Model cards. They contain the names of the people you admire. Put those you admire most at the top. After a while turn over the Model cards, revealing the Keys to their success. Be sure to keep them in order.

- What qualities do you admire most in others?
- Summarize these qualities on a single card.

Are those qualities necessary for you to accomplish your Free Choices? How do they compare to the Summary cards of your strengths in Exercise Two? Are they similar? If they are, it means that you wish to act like the people you admire and that you share a similar drive. Of course, motivation is only one of the necessary ingredients in success. Hard work, talent, and risk-taking are also important. We'll look at them later.

Exercise Four: Statements of Self

Now post all the Summary cards on the board. Look at the person they describe. It is you? Study this board for a while. What do you discover about yourself?

Write each of the following twenty-five statements on its own card and complete them, one at a time, using all the understanding you've just uncovered. Again, it's best to answer quickly, going with the first impression that comes to mind. If you decide to change your answer, put it on a second card and keep it with the first till you're sure.

- I Feel . . .
- I Want . . .
- I Need . . .
- I Dislike . . .

- I Love . . .
- I Aspire to . . .
- I Support . . .
- I'm Addicted to . . .
- I Encourage . . .
- I Doubt . . .
- I Use . . .
- I Accept . . .
- I Dread . . .
- I'm Pulled by . . .
- I Hate . . .
- I Own . . .
- I Discovered . . .
- I Invite . . .
- I Believe . . .
- I Make . . .
- I Give . . .
- I Wish . . .
- I Regret . . .
- I Remember . . .
- I Wish I Could Forget . . .

When you're done, combine these statement cards with the other Summary cards. Carry all these cards around with you for a while. Whenever you have a free moment—waiting at a traffic light, at a coffee break—take out this deck of cards and look at them, but only look at one card at a time. I want you to feel the impact of each statement. Look at them as often as you like. This will help define you, center your energy, and prepare you for outlining your specific goals and risks.

Remember to put any impressions from this exercise in your notebook. They can help as much as the board.

Ted is a thirty-four-year-old florist who is having difficulty with these exercises. All his life he has started projects, only to abandon them at the first hint of failure. Ted's notebook:

Monday: *Feeling uncomfortable with all this soul-searching. I hate looking at these Criticisms. I feel I have taken responsibility for my life! This all feels like old stuff!*

Tuesday: *Couldn't stand working on this! So I didn't.*

Wednesday: *Decided to abandon this entire project!*

Friday: *I looked at my incomplete Action Board and realized that I am abandoning this work in the same way I avoid other problems. The criticisms are right! I got excited about this and decided to stay up all night and fill out the cards. I'm really not as helpless as I lead on to be. It's amazing that I've gotten as far as I have with my crummy attitude. My problem is that I am a quitter! I never admitted that before.*

Again, the way you deal with the Action Board reflects your style of coping with life and planning your future. If you give yourself over to working on these exercises, you are likely to discover why you don't have what you want. And that is a strong beginning in any enterprise.

Keep all the Summary cards on hand for the next section.

Risking: Defining Your Goals

Now you're going to define your goals and consider the steps necessary to reach them.

Because every goal implies a risk and every risk involves a loss, you can't move ahead without leaving something behind. If for the purpose of fortifying yourself you try to convince yourself that everything you're leaving is totally bad and that what you're risking it all for is completely good, you set the scene for disaster. Later, when the going gets rough, the good parts of what you left behind will suddenly loom large and you won't be able to let go. At the moment of risk, when you're about to leap, the impact of the danger you face will finally register. You'll doubt yourself and feel exposed. "Surely," you'll think as you look into the darkness of the unknown, "I'm being hasty. Things can't be all that bad."

Some people fill their lives with unnecessary risking just to create a feeling of urgency in what would otherwise be a dull existence. Take the crisis out of some lives and there isn't anything much to say about them.

And yet every successful life is filled with risks. If you want to get where you have to go, you need to take chances. It's important that you become aware of the loss implied in each risk so you don't lose faith in yourself and abandon the struggle prematurely.

Where Are You Going?

The following exercise requires time and patience. Go slowly and deliberately.

You're going to discover the goals that suit you best, outline the steps needed to reach them, and examine the risks involved in getting there.

For the purpose of this exercise, divide the Action Board into six columns.

Put up the Source cards to the left in column 1. Again, these cards reflect the sources of your pleasure and fulfillment. Look at them and summarize them on a single card; replace them with this summary. Now, turn the Source cards over and summarize the Needs that appear on the back side. Put this summary of Needs directly below the Source card summary in column 1. Combined, these represent your motivations, the forces that move you to act.

Now take the Free Choice summary card you made earlier and post it on the right side of the board in column 6. This indicates where you would head if you were free. This will define your goals.

Just below in column 6, post the summary cards for the Gifts You Gave, the things you were designed to do, the Notions, and also the Improvements you'd like to make in your life. Finally, post the summary card listing the qualities you like in the Models you admire. Taken together, these cards suggest a direction. If you can create an environment that offers these same elements, you stand a high probability of being happy.

In the second column post the summary card for the Obstacles you overcame and below that the summary card for the Deficiencies you corrected.

In the third column post the summary card for the Steps you could take.

In column 4 post your Point of View card, and directly below the summary cards for the Lessons to Learn, Praise, Keys to Success, and Criticisms. Finally, post the Improvement Key summary card in this column as well. This column represents the measure of your actions from several viewpoints and indicates what you must bear in mind when risking. It attempts to define your style of acting.

Column 5 defines your risks. Post a summary of the Excuses you gave for not risking (on the reverse side of the Chance cards) at the top of this column. Filling in the remainder of column 5 with Risks to Take is the purpose of this exercise.

Before you, reading by column from left to right, should be a representation of (1) the forces that motivate you, (2) the obstacles in your path, (3) the steps you might take, (4) your style of acting, and (5) the risks necessary to reach (6) your goals.

Study this board carefully. Consider all of the risks that are necessary for you to move ahead.

Put your responses to the following questions on cards and post them in the Risk column.

- What can you lose?
- Whose affection can you alienate?
- What power or control would you have to give up to get where you want?
- How could you damage your reputation?
- Where are problems most likely to occur?
- Who will be involved? What is important to each of them?
- Do any of the obstacles or deficiencies qualify as future risks in their own right? If so, include them in column 5.
- Judging from column 4, how are you most likely to hurt yourself when risking?
- What risk is most dangerous?
- How can you make it safer?

Using the Tape to Refine the Action Board

Sit in front of the Action Board and replay Tape Three, the Action Board tape. As you listen, simplify, edit, expand, and correct the board. Write additional goals. Rewrite cards to make them easier to understand. If you discover that something important is missing, add it to the board. If you think of a new category that works for you, post it. Be free in dealing with this board. Continually redefine what you want and the risks you need to take. Ask yourself if the cards are accurate. Make the board as truthful and as hopeful as you can. Let its shape take the form of your personality and aspirations.

As you listen to the tape, consider what this person has accomplished, the obstacles he/she overcame, and the ways he/she made himself/herself stronger. If this person used your Action Board as a guide, would it have helped him/her reach the success he/she wanted? Make your board reflect your tape. Be as clear and as simple as possible.

Don't be afraid to dream your dream!

Leave the cards on the board and look at it for at least ten minutes every day for a week. Try to make each card specific. Try to pin down the exact details of each goal. Define what you want, what it leads to, how to get it, and the dangers involved.

This is the Action Board that Deanna, a thirty-three-year-old designer, made just at the point she was deciding to go into business for herself. Notice the high degree of consistency of goals and the drive for a creative life. Notice also how she struggles to believe in herself and her tenacity in overcoming self-doubt. This degree of determination, as well as the self-doubt, is typical of creative, successful people. The consistency of purpose and direction suggest a positive outcome.

Source of Pleasure
Summary

Designing clothes

Creating

Needs

To be free, creative

To express self

Obstacles

Learn to believe in myself

Deficiencies

Learn to make patterns accurately

Learn to draw

Learn to design fabric

Learn how to manage money

Learn to silkscreen

Steps

Return to Design School (Do I know enough?)

Work for designer

Point of View

Truthful—hopeful

Lessons to Learn

Patience

Better organization

Better follow-through

Trust instincts

Praise

I'm original

Criticism

I don't trust myself

Too may diversions

Key to Success

I didn't give up

Improvement Keys

Take one step at a time

Better planning

Excuses

Not good enough

Not deserving

Risks to Take

Find location

Do balance sheets

Design line of clothes

Check other ways of selling

Publicity assistance

Get help

Get financial backing

Danger

Getting in too deep, too quickly

Picking wrong sizes, styles, etc.

Free Choices

To have my own boutique

Gifts I Gave

Things I created

Love and understanding

Notions

To create things

Improvements

Build my own organization/factory

Models I Admire

Originality

Social responsibility

Creativity

At this stage, Deanna's Action Board is repetitive and needs to be simplified. The important point is that she has assembled so many of the critical elements and is now ready to see if she agrees with the direction she has begun to shape.

Making Sure of Your Direction

After a week, when you have refined the board, complete this section.

Look at the board.

- Do you have any doubt about the direction you see indicated before you?
- Is your doubt about the direction or your ability to reach it?

Keep in mind that these directions are only approximate. They are notions of where you think you would like to be, of what you think would make you happy. If all this looks like more than you can handle, consider how realistic you've been in answering the questions that created the board.

- Did you exaggerate your strengths or underestimate your weaknesses?
- What distortions did you permit to interfere with your truthful perception?

Consider again the denial, excuses, and pretenses you used in dealing with the key questions.

- Did these defenses distort your perception of your goals? How?
- Have you denied the impact of some important

loss or failure so that it still overwhelms you, rather than motivates you to change?

- Are you still covering up for your shortcomings instead of growing?
- Has your need to excuse your mistakes made it difficult for you to take responsibility and correct them?
- Have you been so afraid of failing, you pretended you didn't care, and now, just to save face, are you obligated to believe nothing really matters?

Correct your goals from the effect of these defensive distortions.

- What loss must you compensate for?
- What mistakes must you fix?
- What do you really want? What matters to you?

Declare yourself. If you don't, you won't get what you want. You need to come to terms with your direction. Study the board.

- Do you feel capable of achieving the goals represented here?
- Do you feel you deserve to reach them?
- Look at the direction you're heading. Does it feel right? Does it feel like you? Would you be happy if you reached it?
- What other direction could bring the happiness you want?

Remember, your answers will change in time and with experience. Right now you're looking for a general direction that feels right for you. As you study the board consider:

- What is your life's purpose?
- What values do you believe in?
- What needs must you fulfill to be happy?

Look at the life implied by this display. If you don't feel it represents you accurately, correct it.

Don't be dismayed by the amount of work you see ahead of you. If what you wanted wasn't so difficult to attain, you'd already have it. Remember, when you risk for a goal that really matters to you and you have a plan you can believe in, you'll have the courage you need to succeed.

When you remove the cards, note their position, by column and row, so you can reassemble the board when you want.

This is the notebook of Millie, a forty-one-year-old woman who was recently divorced, as she tries to find her goals. Always dependent on her husband, she blamed him for her unhappiness and wasted fifteen years of her life playing cards and complaining.

I ripped all the goals off the board this A.M. I'm disgusted with myself!

It all boils down to realizing that no one is going to take care of me but me. After looking at the board for a week, I see that my only goals lately have been to get even with Robert, to make him pay for leaving me. It seems so stupid to waste my life doing this. I need goals that will please me! All my life I have expected other people to do for me. What I've learned from this board is that all the disappointment in my life has come from depend-

ing on others. I have to let Robert go. It's over.
Punishing him won't do me any good.

The Action Board: Final Stage

In its final stage, the Action Board is a living guide for reshaping your life. Its purpose is to organize this moment along the lines of the goals you've just defined. It is a powerful visual tool to motivate and direct you, and it will give your life a sense of purpose and immediacy. One of the best features of the Action Board is that it gives you such a clear picture of what you need to do next; as a result, when there is nothing to do, you can take time off without feeling guilty.

As I said, I created the Action Board to organize the varied activities of my own life. I usually work on four or five writing projects at once. Each has problems that demand to be evaluated and solved individually. I continually seek new topics for lectures, articles, and for my weekly radio program. I'm always experimenting with new ideas to enhance the effectiveness of psychotherapy, and recently I've been developing some therapeutic applications for computers. In all, I work on fifteen to twenty separate concepts, each evolving at a different pace, and it would be impossible to keep them all current without this organizational help. My Action Board is easy to maintain. It visualizes the progress of each project and tells me when to act and where.

My first attempt to create this system seemed to dishearten me by making me aware of all the loose ends in my life. Once I got over the shock, I began to streamline my projects, to concentrate on what really mattered, and to let go of what was clearly never going to be. Over the years I developed the following system, which I believe will be of great help to you.

Remember, creating an effective Action Board takes time. It evolves slowly and becomes more refined, more pertinent, and more realistic as you continue to use it. My board always gets simpler. While the Action Board that you are creating will be effective and revealing, the one that it will evolve into in a few months will be clearer and even more meaningful and helpful. And that won't begin to compare with the one you'll have a year from now.

Assembling Your Final Action Board

TITLING EACH CARD

First, collect all the cards you created in the previous sections and separate out all the Goals you defined. They may come from any column, notebook, or tape. By this time you should realize that creating Tape Three was merely a device to open you up to the possibility of becoming your best. If you didn't make the tape or complete the board exercises, you should make a list of all your goals or projects. Put down every possibility. Don't make any judgment about your goals at this stage. Summarize each goal in a few words and write it as a title across the top half of a 3-by-5 card. Print it in large letters so you can read the goal from across the room. Each card is to serve as a flag to signal your awareness, bringing you into focus, setting your mind to work. If you wish, you can use an entire wall as your display space, as some people do, especially when they are just beginning to narrow down their choices from a large number of possibilities. Date every card, both when you post it on the board and when you take it down. Place your Immediate Goals on the left, the Intermediate Goals in the middle, and the Long-Term Goals on the right.

GROUPING

When all your Goals are posted, sit back at a little distance and look at the display.

Can you arrange your goals in groups? Try doing so.

Do some goals seem to be part of the same growth process, and do they, therefore, share the same risks? It's important to know what is at stake in each risk you take. If you're aware of what your success depends on, you're more likely to be decisive. People hesitate most when they're caught off guard by a risk they didn't expect.

Do some goals depend on or follow close behind others? If so, put them in order, with the first goal at the top of each group. Try to be aware of the context of each goal and its relationship to others so you can anticipate opportunities and are prepared to act when they appear. In this way you create and sustain momentum toward your greater goal. Knowing where you're going gives you the confidence you need.

The following are card titles from the Action Board of Betty, a brilliant twenty-three-year-old who works in a department store and is trying to decide what to do with her life. Because of a depressed economy, she took a job for security and now finds herself chewing at the bit, wishing to be in a more challenging position but still lacking courage to risk. She needs a plan.

Reading List (escape from reality?)

Ask for meeting with my supervisor. (Get design position or quit?)

New job possibilities
Publishing (Call Tina Wilson in N.Y.)

Film editing (need to read about this)

Translator (you'd get bored)

Teacher (ugh)

Diary as novel (it's been done!)

Design set of dishes

Talk to Wanda about designing wallpaper (Peter's father is in the business)

Posters for kids

A children's book

Start your own business!

Buy large sketchbook. Sketch ideas.

Her Notebook:

I'd like to start my own design studio someday. But competition is tough! I can see how slow business is in the store.

Maybe I should create designs and license other people to manufacture them. How would I start? Where would I sell the products?

I know that the company I work for wants me to stay as head of housewares because I'm so good in sales, but I want to design! I should talk to Peter's dad.

I have too many "shoulds" in my life. I must "do"!

I must contact people in creative fields and find out how they did it.

Betty is tough on herself, but very determined. Her wide range of interests is typical of young people in general and creative people in particular. She needs a single focus. More than that, she needs more experience trying out various interests so she can see what she likes doing. Too much of her planning is theory. She needs some hands-on experience.

Opening Yourself to Your Creative Process

Once more, your Action Board is a reflection of yourself. At best, it is dynamic and ever-changing. It requires careful pruning and shaping. Feel free to add, correct, or remove subjects. Make it an extension of the way you think. If an idea comes to mind, put it on the board. You should continually be adding possible goals and ideas to your Action Board.

A life that is truly alive is lived in process; that means it is open to creation, innovation, and growth. New ideas will come to you when they feel welcome in your presence. That may sound far-fetched, but the metaphor is correct. To encourage new ideas, make a habit of writing them down whenever they occur. Carry blank 3-by-5 cards with you just for this purpose. Also, never make judgments about a new idea's worth. Just write it down. Your creative self is highly sensitive to criticism. It wants to improvise and shuts off when you correct it. So save your correcting for later. Further, it's not a good idea to force your creativity. You'll only be disappointed with the results. To attain a spontaneous state of reception, put yourself at the disposal of the ideas that naturally flow through you and take the time to capture them as they occur. If you define your problems openly, the answers will come close behind.

Remember, suspend judgment when you are creating. It's critical to the flow of the process.

WEEDING

At this time, remove any project that you strongly feel doesn't belong on your Action Board. Be realistic, but don't throw an idea away because it looks like a lot of work or because you're afraid of the risk. Your wish to push some subject away may be the greatest obstacle you face in reaching your goal.

Look at the board again. Is there something missing? Always ask that question when you look at the board. If you come up with an answer, write it down and post it.

Your Card File

This is optional, but helpful. It's a good idea to save all of the cards you remove from the board in a 3-by-5 card file with labeled dividers. For example, file the cards you've weeded out under the heading Rejected Goals. These files will help you maintain a sense of continuity. When you're uncertain of your direction, looking at where you've been sometimes provides the answer. Set up a section in the card file for each goal you decide to keep on the board.

This may seem like a lot of paperwork in the beginning and that's true, for at every beginning there's always more work. But if you take the time and follow this model, you will find the system easy to maintain and well worth the effort. The file system will keep your important ideas in context.

It's also helpful to keep a section in your file labeled Trial Goals, for ideas often first appear as incomplete fragments. Keeping them on file allows you to review them and create a better concept later on. All this may seem complicated, but it's not. Once you set up this system it builds its own momentum and becomes easier to use.

Information to Keep Close at Hand

After you've assembled your first set of goals on the board, you're ready to write on the cards in the space below each title. Use this space to store important information, such as the names and telephone numbers of the people involved in the project, critical reminders, or dates. This keeps you mindful of important details and brings key people one step closer. In general, use this space for the information you'd want an assistant to have handy. Don't clutter these spaces with information you've already memorized, but put down information that is routinely needed in implementing the project.

The Next Step

When you have completed your Action Board, each of your Goals will have a second card immediately below it. That will define the Next Step you must take toward reaching your goal.

Take care in preparing these Next Steps, for they are the most important device in this method. Taken together, they tell what you should be doing to get where you want. It is at this collection of steps that you will risk failure, reach success, and find happiness. They monitor your growth, reveal your future, and reaffirm your belief in yourself. If you design these Next Step cards honestly, they will create progress, inspire hope, and motivate you to work.

Take each Goal individually and using everything

you know, write out all the steps you'll have to take to reach it, putting each one on its own 3-by-5 card. You may also wish to indicate what the success of each step depends on and make note of any potential danger in taking it.

Arrange these steps in the most logical order and post them below the Goal so you can see them all at once.

A CHECKLIST FOR EACH STEP

Your object now is to decide which step is *the* Next Step. Consider the following:

- Are you sure about the order of the steps? Rearrange them till you're satisfied.
- Which steps are dangerous?
- What can go wrong? Where, when, how, with whom?
- How can you prevent it? Even if you can't prevent it, just being aware that there is a rough spot up ahead will prepare you.
- Who can help you?
- With whom should you share this?
- How important is each step in attaining your goal?

When you decide on a final order, choose the step that you believe is next and post it immediately beneath its Goal on the Action Board. If two or three steps seem to be equal, pin them all up and test them out together. It's the best way to learn. File the other steps, keeping them in order.

Be creative and flexible in what you put down for the Next Step. Let the steps fit the work you do. Some Next Steps on my Action Board indicate a person to contact and a question to ask. Some are writing tasks, such as "Outline scenes" or "Rewrite case histories."

One is an encouraging sign beneath a project in its infancy, cheering, "Keep this up." One goal I'm still doubtful about has "Do you really want to do this?" posted beneath. Another Next Step describes a potential investment. Some contain trial outlines of new projects, and still others say, "Has this been done before?" or "If no reply by the first, take manuscript back."

I continually test the validity of all my Next Steps. I feel perfectly comfortable staring at the same Next Step for six months without acting on it, although I might add a word here or there from time to time. After a while I'll call the person whose name is on the title card and discuss it. Then I'll either have a new impetus to develop the idea further or a good reason to abandon it.

In examining each of your Goals and determining the appropriate Next Step, take all the time you need. It may be weeks before you have completed all the Next Steps for every Goal on the board. You don't need to spend endless hours at this. As I said, once you start, the board will take on a momentum of its own and a few minutes a day will be sufficient. Each time you look at the board you'll see another possibility. New ideas will blossom. You'll start solving problems and your situation will improve. Just having an Action Board in view introduces a powerful directive force into your life.

One lady, a friend of a patient of mine, kept a primitive and disorganized Action Board on her refrigerator door in imitation of my patient. She was surprised to realize suddenly what she should be doing with her life. The board had been organizing her thinking while she cooked for her family.

Looking for Trouble Spots

When all your Goals have a Next Step pinned beneath them, reconsider what each step depends on for success and the risks involved as well as any potential danger. Put these Cautions down on a card in a few words, such as "Pay attention to" or "Look out for."

These Caution cards depict the danger of this moment. Studying them after you've accumulated a few will be revealing.

In fact, after a while, everything you put up on this board will have a story to tell. It is valuable to spread out all the previous steps of a single project when analyzing a particular problem in detail. Keeping the right perspective is critical.

I organize my Action Board so that the least active goals are kept on the left and the most pressing are on the right. This keeps me focused on what's most important and still mindful of the least active goal. In fact, I recently brought to life a goal that had occupied the least active position for six years merely because the board kept me aware of it.

Remember, the object of the board is to create a grid of signposts that reflect your intention and continually redirect your creative process along the lines that serve you best.

Your Intention

The Action Board reveals your direction. The Next Steps remind you of your immediate intention. You create the opportunity to act by preparing and expecting it to present itself. There are many keys to success, but none is more important than defining your intention.

To intend is the active verb of the mind. Your intention manifests itself when the opportunity arises. Your intent is not always pure. As you know by now, when your unmet needs shape your intentions, you're capable of behavior that goes against your best interests.

The Action Board will help you identify your best intentions and prime you to act on the opportunities that continually present themselves, but you still must feel deserving to take advantage of them in the brief moment that action is possible. If you follow the guidelines we've covered for expressing your feelings, you can free your intention from these self-destructive forces and make your life whatever you want it to be.

If you don't, you won't be happy.

Your Action Board is now ready to evolve. Look at it each day. Let it influence you. If you hit a snag or need inspiration for new ideas, play Tape III again.

The power you seek is found by knowing that *you* must save yourself. There is strength in recognizing that you are the defender of your life. There is a simple elegance to the logic of all this. It is based on the truth

If you aren't going to save yourself, you aren't going to be saved. No one else can save you, except momentarily. It's true, someone may pull you out of danger, provided they are there when you get into trouble and notice and care enough to risk on your behalf, but most of the time your battle will be a lonely one. You do best to look out for yourself because even if someone does answer your call for help, he or she still won't be able to save you the way you could've saved yourself if you'd accepted responsibility and prepared.

> *Life always catches up with you.*
> *Your power is in accepting this.*
> *This acceptance fortifies your intent.*
> *Your intention spawns your actions.*
> *You become your actions.*

The Action Board will grow with you and help you achieve what you pursue if your goals are honest. It cannot make unrealistic goals a reality. It cannot give you the voice of a Metropolitan Opera star, the literary style of Ernest Hemingway, or the beauty of a fashion model, but it can help you define and bring out the inner beauty of your own life. The Action Board can give you a perspective on your ability and help you understand the work that is involved in developing it. It can help you become your best by letting you see what is in your way. By defining your path, it helps you make progress toward your goals.

Why pine your life away, wishing to be what you're not, when finding the best you are will be more than enough to make you happy?

The person you are now becoming lives within you. If it is your irrevocable intention that your best self will predominate and manifest itself in your actions, you will find the courage to begin and the strength to complete the necessary work to get what you want.

There is no easy way to do all of this. The Action Board is a valuable tool, but the effort must be yours.

The secret of life is that there is no secret of life. It is all hard work. If you can find the work that nurtures you, it will make you whole. You are your best when you're giving the most. You give the most to a cause you believe in.

Your passion for living depends on this.

Marathon Exercises: Checking Your Progress (Six Months After Section Six)

This exercise is a review of all the work you've done on your Action Board in the past six months. The object is to assess your progress and reconsider your direction.

You'll need an entire afternoon or evening to complete the exercise. Replay Tape III. Sit in front of your Action Board as you listen; take notes and revise. Consider the following questions as you work, measure your progress, and examine your direction in light of them.

TIMING

- Have you acted when you should?
- Did you miss opportunities? Why?
- How did you prepare for important events?
- What forces made you act?
- What forces still hold you back?
- How long did it take you to realize that something wasn't working out?
- How much time did you waste? When?
- When did you act rashly?
- When were you afraid of testing yourself? Why?
- When will you take your next risk?

TALENT

- What missing skills still stand in your way?
- What education or training do you need now?
- What talents must you develop?
- Have you given yourself the support you need?
- What has gotten in your way?
- Why have you permitted it to stop you?

EFFORT

- How hard have you worked?
- Have you worked on the right problems?

- When do you do your best work?
- Do you try to work then?
- When are you most likely to give up?
- How can you improve your work habits?
- Do you feel deprived when you work?
- Are you working at something that really matters to you?
- How important is luck to your success?
- Do you trust your accomplishments or do you feel they can be taken away from you?
- How sincere has your effort been? Have you coasted along, avoiding conflicts, or have you risked?

ATTITUDE

- How has your outlook changed?
- Are you afraid of what lies ahead?
- How deserving do you feel?
- How can you act more positively?
- Will you succeed?
- How sure are you?

As you ponder these questions, realize that they may not be answerable at this time. They are meant to help you update your Action Board. The Action Board is your palette. You are the artist. Your job is to create your best life. That work is always continuing. It's that work that keeps you alive, that keeps you young.

Growth is the balm of life.

Follow-up Instructions

The progress we have made together in this book is just the beginning. Keep your Action Board up to date. Look at it every day for a few minutes, and every other month, spend an hour or two updating the cards, reconsidering their position on the board. Weed, edit, update, add.

Allow the Action Board to assume a place of prominence in your planning and thinking. It will repay you many times over for any effort you expend. Remember, the purpose of the Action Board is not to write cards but to develop understanding, and while I have given you instructions on how to proceed, the various examples should tell you that there is no set way. You must adapt this plan to fit your own situation.

It's a good idea to replay Tape I in a year to see how your ideas have changed.

Making a new Feeling Tape in a year and comparing it with the original one is valuable, too. You'll be fascinated with the way you've grown in dealing with emotions as well as how the issues that affect you change. You don't need to make a lengthy Feeling Tape. Taking a brief inventory of your feelings during a three-day period should be enough to make the comparison.

As you've seen, replaying Tape III is a useful way of taking an inventory of the Action Board and reviewing goals.

It's also an excellent practice to tape and routinely replay arguments, planning sessions, improvisations, diary entries, discussions, and any other important meetings. You'll discover more about the way you are and what you miss when others talk to you.

7 | Some Last Thoughts

Acting from Strength

The purpose of this book has been to help you find your true center, the place from which you act as yourself. Centered people know who they are and what they feel. They are not afraid of being seen. They know where they have been and what forces formed them, and they are free to respond spontaneously. They know where they're going; they have the courage of their convictions and the belief in themselves to follow through.

They know they are good.

By contrast, uncentered people operate from the fringe of their defenses. They don't want you to see or touch them. They keep you at a distance. You don't feel free talking with them because they twist what you say to fit their beliefs. They won't let you be you because they don't feel good about being themselves. They act impulsively or for show, reflexively defending what they incompletely understand. Because they refuse to analyze their decisions, they are unlikely to grow. They insist that they are always right, and should you attempt to correct them, they become consumed with making you wrong. They want so badly to believe they are safe, that they are in constant danger.

Uncentered people spend their lives hoping, not planning. They hide from pain until it becomes impossible to ignore. Then, if they are not paralyzed by unexpressed feelings, they desperately try to catch up. Of course, when time is running out and pressures are intense, the threat of failure is greatest. The crisis atmosphere that clings to such people doesn't lend itself to reflecting or problem solving, but to automatic or escapist behavior.

Understandably, these people have difficulty reconciling their unrealistic expectations with the world. They dismiss what they cannot understand as crazy, presumptuous, or unworthy of being taken seriously and try to discredit any bearer of bad news. They seem to labor constantly, but it's largely defensive work. They struggle to keep their frontiers intact and feel obligated to quarrel with anyone they perceive as a threat. Because they are constantly on the alert, they feel exhausted. They cannot flow comfortably with events because they're committed to proving the world is the way they see it. The more they defend against life, the farther from their center they stand. This rigidity is their ruin.

One of the ways you can tell you're dealing with centered people is that you feel comfortable being yourself in their presence, for they have no need to change or manipulate others. They accept people because they accept themselves.

Because centered people are at peace, you can't get them to lose control. They react to you from deep within. They can listen and watch from a distance. So when you act provocatively, they're likely to let it be your problem.

Centered people don't waste time looking for approval. They may ask your opinion of a difficult situation, not for reassurance, but to get your perspective on an elusive reality. They operate by feelings, trust their feelings, and handle them at the point they originate and with the person who caused them. They take responsibility for their actions and settle their business of the moment in the moment it occurs.

Centered people do not carry excess emotional baggage. They continually shed what they have outgrown. They stay vital by being open to change and growth. They deal with experience freshly, without invoking the past to justify their actions. They don't insist on being right. They bear no grudge and live without blame or apology. They do what they think is best, when they want to. They trust themselves and act without ambivalence.

People who are centered are people who are free. They owe nothing and want only what they deserve. They are realists who understand that they can only be what they are. They give you all the room you need to be yourself, including giving you enough rope to hang yourself. They stand out of your way, neither claiming nor possessing you. All they desire is the room to be themselves. If you look closely, they have already taken it.

Being Happy, Being You

A free person is a happy person. Helping you find a freer, more honest way to live your life is my objective. It is not an easy task, and the growing that lies ahead will keep you awake. A happy life is full of discovery and challenge, of risks and fulfillment. You must earn your keep every day.

Getting what you want requires that you *give* all you can.

Your work should be a celebration of the best you can be, and you should always be getting better. Your commitment to this is the only source of hope you can trust.

When you are positive, you become filled with energy and life has meaning. If you are true to the belief that you are good and deserve to have good things happen to you, you expand to become your belief. It is only when you fill yourself that you can give without measure, for you become as much as you give.

There may not be a grand plan, but there most certainly is an equalizing balance. Time tells the ultimate truth. What works lives on.

In these pages I have tried to direct your eye inward to examine the forces that shaped you and the feelings through which you experience life in order to help you unlock the dreams hidden in your heart. My goal has been to give you the courage to risk being yourself. There is nothing as important as being free, and you can be free the moment you accept responsibility for everything in your life.

This age has been labeled as one preoccupied with the self. Perhaps it is, but that is not necessarily bad. A world populated by people who reach for their best is the better world we should all seek. At some point you must make a leap of faith and declare, "I am good and I love myself." You must believe that and act as if it were true.

Acting on the belief you are good is being your best.

If you are at peace with yourself, you can appreciate the world around you.

If you love yourself, you can love others.

Accept and be yourself just as you are and build on it. Then you'll believe that life is going to get better.

And it will.

Appendix

Meditation Exercises

The following exercise is a model for meditation. It is a composite of several classical techniques. It's useful for inducing a state of relaxation and also for making contact with the source of energy within you. This energy is the life force. Contacting it produces a feeling of renewal and peace.

Sit quietly with your legs crossed and breathe deeply and slowly. Close your eyes and keep them closed throughout the meditation. *Silently* repeat the words "I am" over and over again throughout the exercise, using the sound of the words to block your thoughts. Every time an idea or a sensation starts to appear, focus your attention on repeating "I am."

Even though you may feel awkward, continue to repeat "I am" to yourself. In a few minutes you will feel a calming effect.

Yield to the thoughtlessness of this state.

Anticipate something appearing behind your forehead.

It may not happen the first few times, but after a while an elusive, beautiful blue spot appears. Keep it in view. What is inside the blue? It is the energy that spawns all knowing and being, bound in your body as your life, released at death, to be reunited again with its source.

What is that source? You can only guess, for you cannot know on such a scale. You can only attempt to be one with this energy that is in all things. Perhaps it is no more or less complicated than a single electron orbiting the nucleus of a hydrogen atom. It is found in the most distant celestial object and in the nearest handful of topsoil. It fosters every bright hope of mankind and every yearning for peaceful survival in a world of friends. Each of us sustains part of the same life force as our mutual endowment. Your imperative is to make yourself free so it can work through you. Although you cannot know that greater energy, you can still participate in it by being in harmony with the part of it that touches you and gives you life.

Your intention is to go through the blue spot. You do this by yielding, letting go of all thought, keeping the blueness as your goal, and repeating "I am" as you try to reach the blue spot, for it is the seat of your highest consciousness. It stands at the interface between the world without and the world within. It is where you experience being, beyond reflection. It is the place in your mind where you are aware only of your energy flowing, without adornment, explanation, or self-consciousness.

Because attaining the blue spot is accomplished without words, without the distorting effect of the mind, it is an excellent metaphor for experiencing your inner self at your tranquil best. Trying to reach the blue spot strengthens your ability to focus on your mental energy.

It's a good practice to do this once a day for fifteen to twenty minutes, preferably after arising or at sunset. But you can meditate once or twice a week or even less often with positive results. Meditating accustoms you to find and tap the source of your inner strength. It brings a feeling of oneness and peace to your life and has done so for millions of people for thousands of years.

Once you have become accustomed to reaching the blue spot, you can quickly do so anytime you wish simply by closing your eyes and repeating "I am" to yourself. You will feel a surge of energy and perhaps a momentary lightheadedness. Relax, open your eyes, let the feeling go, and return to your efforts with renewed control and energy. It's a good way to approach a stressful situation, release tension, or to initiate creative thinking.

Simply repeating "I am" aloud also has considerable power to center you; that is, to free you from extraneous influences. Repeat it for a minute or so, but in this case be mindful of its meaning. It is especially useful when you feel anxious or unsettled.

Meditations

These pieces are intended to keep you in the right frame of mind, to help you find yourself when you feel confused, and to give you courage by putting you in touch with your best.

Read them for reassurance and strength.

Read each piece aloud slowly. Then close your eyes and think about the thought.

I

You are privileged.
You are endowed with life.
The purpose of life is to celebrate life, to create and
    sustain living things.
Give to that purpose the force of your belief.
Then your world will be yours.
It's up to you.
It has always been.
The life without mirrors the life within.

II

You never know for whom you toil,
Who will reap the benefit of your work,
Who will grow in the nurturing of your giving,
Or who will respond to your being or having been.
All you can do is commit to a dream,
Work hard,
And act like someone who is the way you want to
    be.

III

I create my life.
I am master of this world I see.
No bounds knows my spirit.
No prison any tyranny.
Except the bonds that hold my feelings captive
And make me slave to time and injury past.
Only I can imprison me.
Only I can set me free.

IV

I am the power within.
What I see when my eyes are closed is me.
This other world, energy uncontaminated by
    thought,
Is the source of my strength.
I am intention becoming me.
I intend good.
I am good.
I know that good will flow from me.

V

I am not my body.
I am the energy that gives flesh life.
I have settled down within me for a time.
I seek to do the work I have to do.
My purpose is being.
My being is doing.
I am my best when I am giving of me.

VI

Be your best.
Let your energy free to feel, to be.
Love yourself.
Everything depends on it.
To find yourself just be yourself.
Take your life seriously or your life will be taken
    from you.
You must go on.
No matter what has been or can be,
You must overcome this moment to move on.

You're going to make it if you work at it,
So act in accordance with that belief.
Now is the time for your best effort.
Risk when you're most likely to succeed.

VII

Believe in yourself
Especially when you're down,
Even when there's no reason,
Even when it's darkest,
Even when it's hopeless.
Your belief is the answer.
Your belief is the reason you'll succeed.
Your belief is the difference.

VIII

I am the whole world looking out my eyes.
I am myself,
Free to feel, think, or be.
Because I am free,
I am completely me.
And because I am so honestly me,
I am also you.

IX

You become what you imagine yourself to be.
Most of your problems come from your fear of
   being alone.
Your joy and punishment is that you have to live
   your life as yourself.

Until you begin the journey of becoming your best,
   you cannot be happy.
The way you are is the way your world becomes.
Expect good to happen and good will find you.
Live your life so the truth is your friend.
Be full for yourself.
Learn the lesson of every loss, and your suffering
   won't repeat.
For the pain of mourning is the burden of regret.
To expect to grow is to remain forever young.

Additional Exercises to Resolve Anxiety

Breathing Exercise

The following exercises are beneficial. Use them as
often as you like.

Sit in a quiet place, preferably on a cushion with your
legs crossed, your hands resting quietly in your lap.

Breathe slowly and deeply. As you inhale, think, *"I
fill up with strength and peace."* Hold your breath. As
you exhale, think, *"I let fear flow out of me."*

Repeat this ten times with your eyes closed.

Meditation

Read aloud slowly and repeat three times.

I am complete.
I have all the strength I need.
Nothing will take me before my time.
Fear does not hold me.
I let fear go.
It passes through me, a wave spent upon the sand.
I intend peace.
Within me peace.

Imaging Exercise

Read over the following guide until you are familiar with its contents, then sit quietly with your eyes closed and breathe easily. Allow your mind to go blank and go through the exercise.

Imagine yourself by a peaceful woods facing a lake. Everywhere you look you see comfort and tranquillity. It is late afternoon. The light is soft and the air is still. You are looking across the glassy lake with the perfect reflection of a mountain on the other side. Place yourself here and look about, noticing details: flowers, trees, and birds.

Able to move great distances just by wishing, you imagine yourself floating up to a mountain meadow at the edge of the timberline. You stand on the gentle slope. The air is clear and warm. The moment feels as free as an afternoon in childhood. You look across the valley below at the light-streaked clouds drifting by.

You notice a mossy path and follow it along a gurgling stream until you come to a pool with large boulders all about. You look into the pool and see your face reflected clearly. You look serene. The more you look at your peaceful face, the calmer you feel. Just ahead, you see the opening of a cave with an intense golden light coming from within. As you enter the cave, the light seems to pass through you, warming you and filling you with peace.

As you stand in this warm energy you feel lighter. You feel yourself soaring free of all earthly bonds through the golden clouds. Away . . . free.

Hold on to this moment as long as you can.

Every time you wish to release yourself from the grip of fear, repeat these exercises. You can also invent other elements to strengthen you, such as finding powerful trinkets and charms in other parts of the cave. Or a kind sage who lives at the far end of the cave, who will answer all your questions. Ask him; you'll see.

Imagine that you are touching the source of your own power whenever you immerse yourself in the golden light.

Always start the exercise by placing yourself in the woods by the lake and then soaring to the mountain. Look into the pool expecting to see your reflection at peace. Enter the cave to be energized in its golden rays.

This healing energy is within you, and these exercises are but a symbolic path to release it.

Showing Appreciation

In case you haven't noticed, you had help getting where you are. Hardly anyone does it on their own. It's important to show appreciation for the gifts you've received, the good advice, the calming words, the kind thoughts, the loving support, and the honest appraisals.

Too many people are embarrassed by the idea of thanking others. Perhaps it's their shame over being in such need in the first place that makes them shy away from showing appreciation. Let me reassure you, a word of appreciation—brief, to the point, sincere, and appropriate—is the best way to repay a kindness. It's also good manners. Being recognized for the good they've done is enough of a reward for most people, and anything less is often a source of hurt. When you acknowledge another person's giving, you become part of it. Your thanks encourage the triumph of caring over indifference.

Even if you've never won or feel bitter about not getting a break, there are people on your side who have tried to help. Someone deserves to hear from you and needs to know that you noticed.

Who are the people who have helped you?

Whose giving has made a difference in your life?

Here are some letters I've written to friends who have helped me.

Dear Jonah,
Some of the best advice I ever got, I got from you. You are a valued friend and a dear soul.

Dear Eric,
Thank you for holding my hand and putting up with me when I've been impossible. It's been more than a job for you, it's been a mission.

Dear Katharine,
Thank you for loving me and making me lovable when even I couldn't stand myself.

Dear Arthur,
Your support and positive outlook always make a difference.

Just before mailing your appreciations, post them on your Action Board to remind yourself of your good fortune.

Glossary

Alone The natural state of every living being or thing; not a state of need

Apathy Making everything meaningless to avoid being judged

Attitude Pattern of choices

Belief Knowing that something is so (whether or not it is)

Blame To seek external reasons

Boredom Missing the thread of life; answered fleetingly by sex; solved by the act of creating and self-acceptance

Bravery Knowing you can handle your feelings

Closed A defensive position based on the belief that one is bad

Closeness Being alone together

Comfortable Able to cope with the feelings of a particular reality

Commitment Mutuality of purpose

Competitive Fear of testing the self directly

Controlling Fear of being free projected onto others

Courage Belief in the necessity of a thing

Cowardice Using fear as an excuse

Crazy (1) Holding on to pain; (2) Believing in something everyone else immediately recognizes as false; (3) Acting self-destructively, believing the opposite

Critical Mildest form of blame

Curiosity Urgency to know; heightened by the fear of loss or injury

Defense A pattern of thought or behavior, transient or ingrained, that serves to protect a person from pain, real or imagined, in the present or the past

Dependence The natural state of children; in adults, the belief that being oneself is not enough

Despair Abandonment of hope

Distortion Any alteration of reality to fit a particular need

Doubt Avoidance of knowing

Embarrassment Disclosure of deficiencies

Envy The belief that in order to be complete you need what others have

Expectation The anticipation of a belief

Feeling The primary sensation of being; the direct experience of existence

Forgive To concede that your pain has passed

Generosity The expression of feeling complete

Giving Expressing self-love

Happy Liking the way you feel

Hope Trusting that something is so

Identity What you imagine yourself to be

Independence Assuming the mantle of personhood

Insincerity Getting away with as much as you can

Irritation Anger's first flush

Jealous The belief you are replaceable

Knowing The truth from a certain perspective

Lonely Missing part of oneself; usually mistakenly projected on some external object

Love Caring about the feelings of another as if they were your own

Manipulative Acting to control the outcome; afraid to be honest

Mourn To express anger over a loss

Need An incompleteness of self

Obsession A trapped feeling seeking expression as thoughts

Open Willing to grow, be seen, to see, based on self-acceptance

Paranoia The loneliness of not feeling acceptable, projected onto the world

Patience The belief you are on the right track

Peace of mind Knowing you did what you had to do

Personality An individual style of dealing with feelings

Possessive The belief that you need another person

Prejudice In search of evidence

Reality The subjective integration of sensations and thoughts both felt and remembered; varies from moment to moment, person to person

Realization Seeing the old anew

Release No longer being injured

Resistance Postponing the truth

Rich Needing nothing

Sanity When what is good for you makes you happy and you can act to get it

Secrecy Fear of sharing

Self-pity Extending the reaction time between being hurt and showing anger; using being hurt as a weapon

Stress The pressure of unexpressed feelings seeking release

Strong people Those who can do what they want when they need to

Suggestible Dependent on external directives to the exclusion of feelings

Suspicious Wary of evil

Therapy Any process that helps you give up false beliefs

Time The belief in the importance of two events; the primary measure of space; the distance between then and now

Trust To risk being hurt

Utopia A place where it is easy to tell what is real from what is not

Waiting Lack of anything to do

Whole Committed to the moment

Will Singlemindedness of intention

Working through Dealing with emotions so the smallest residue remains

Follow-up

Because we've shared so much in these pages, I'd like to know more about your response to this book, how you benefited, and how you felt it could have been more helpful. I would be grateful for any feedback you could provide. If you send a postcard to David Viscott, *c/o* Houghton Mifflin Company, 2 Park Street, Boston, Massachusetts 02108, I'll send you a questionnaire that will help me evaluate your progress and be more responsive to your needs in the future.